Science
Olympiad

Class 07

A must have book for all
Olympiads & Talent Search Exams...

by
Deepti Pillai

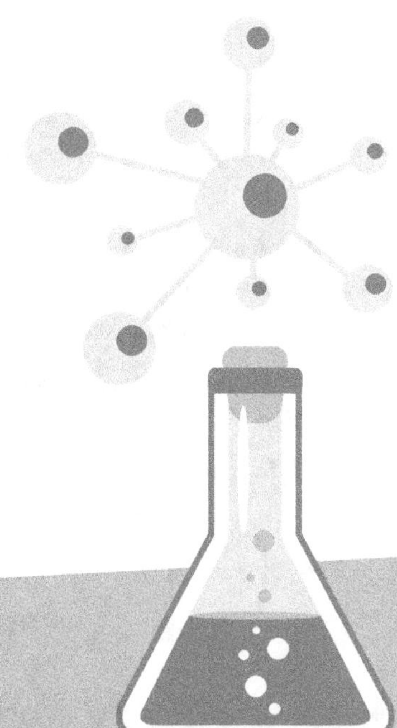

BLOOM CAP
Bloom Cap Edu Ventures Pvt. Ltd.

Bloom Cap Edu Ventures Pvt. Ltd.

❀ **Administrative & Production Office**

'Ramchhaya' 4577/15, Agarwal Road, Darya Ganj, New Delhi -110002
Tele: 011- 47630600, 43518550

❀ **ISBN :** 978-93-25519-36-7

❀ **PRICE :** ₹100.00

❀ **PO No :** TXT-XX-XXXXXXX-X-XX

For further information about the books log on to
www.bloomcap.org

Follow us on   

Preface

"Future belongs to those Who prepares for it today"

School Olympiads are National & International level competitions conducted by different Government, Non-Government & Educational Organisations with the purpose of making the children ready to face competitive exams.

The challenging Questions asked in Olympiads motivate them to learn more & more and bring out the best result with improved academic performance. The Awards & Scholarship offered by Olympiads motivate children to aspire & strive for doing better and emerge out to be the best.

Science Olympiads

Being a Scientist or Engineer or Doctor has always been a dream of each school going child. A good command over Science is a must for any of these. Questions of Science Olympiads are structured to help students to develop scientific temperament & motivate them to understand the concepts of science. They also focuses on improving existing knowledge of a student by adding more information.

'Bloom Science Olympiad Study Book Class 7' is a perfect resource to Study & Practice for Olympiad Exams and other National & State Level Talent Search Exams & Other Competitions.

Some Special Features of Bloom Science Olympiad Study Books are;

- Chapterwise Exercises having different types of Objective Questions; Analytical, Applications, Remembering etc, at par with the Olympiad Level.
- Detailed Explanation for each question.
- Olympiad Pattern Practice Sets at the end.

This book is prepared by Expert Panel with the utmost care, still if you have any suggestions regarding its improvement then feel free to contact us at olympiads@bloomcap.org. We will try to inculcate your suggestions in the further editions.

Contents

Nutrition in Plants

1 Mark Questions

1. The solid arrows in the diagram given below represent the direction of movement of substances P and Q when photosynthesis is taking place in a leaf.

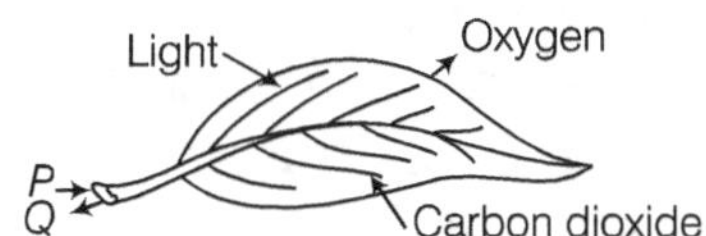

What are P and Q ?

	P	Q
(a)	Water	Sugar
(b)	Starch	Sugar
(c)	Sugar	Starch
(d)	Water	Oxygen

2. The following equation represents the process in photosynthesis.

$$6CO_2 + 6H_2O \xrightarrow[\text{energy}]{\text{Sunlight}} C_6H_{12}O_6 + 6O_2$$

From your understanding of this process, if radioactive oxygen (^{18}O) was incorporated into water. Which of the following substances will contain ^{18}O?
   (a) Oxygen   (b) Glucose
   (c) Water   (d) Carbon dioxide

3. Pick out the correct name and function of part X in the figure given below from the options that follow.

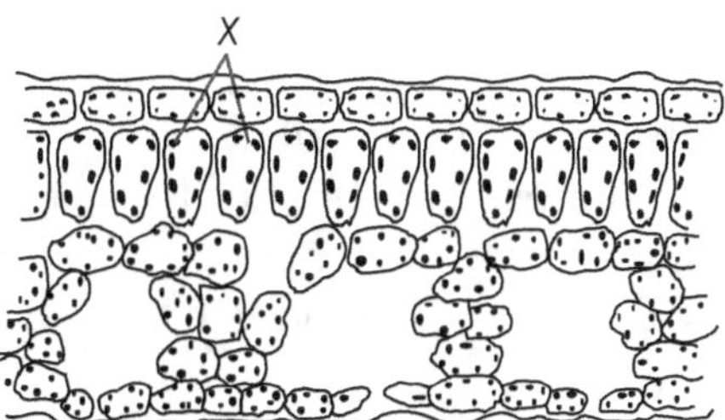

   A. Provide chemical energy.
   B. Allow gaseous exchange.
   C. Regulate rate of transpiration.
   D. Conduct photosynthesis by absorbing sunlight.
   1. Stoma
   2. Chlorophyll
   3. Guard cells
   4. Chloroplast

   Mark the correct match.
   (a) 1–B   (b) 2–C
   (c) 4–D   (d) 3–B

4. In plants who derive nutrition by trapping different insects, the leaves have been modified as
   (a) leaf tendrils   (b) spines
   (c) pitchers   (d) fleshy leaves

5. Complete the analogy given below.

Cuscuta : Parasite : : *Rhizopus* : X
   (a) Insectivore
   (b) Symbiotic partner
   (c) Saprophyte
   (d) Lichen

6. A bird sets on the back of a rhino. The bird receives food in form of worms or insects, while the rhino gets rid of parasites. This relationship can be identified as
   (a) saprotrophism
   (b) symbiosis
   (c) totally parasitic where worms and insects are parasites
   (d) partial parasitism where only bird receives nutrition

7. 'Fungi are often called as decomposers. Which of the characterstics of these organisms given below is responsible for this ability?
   (a) They feed on insects
   (b) They feed on dead and decaying organic matter
   (c) They feed on plants
   (d) They receive nutrients from a host's body

8. The symbiotic relationship between the bacteria *Rhizobium* and a leguminous host plant is correctly defined as
   (a) *Rhizobium* fixes atmospheric nitrogen for self-nutrition.
   (b) *Rhizobium* provides food and shelter to the host plants.
   (c) Atmospheric N_2 is converted into soluble form by *Rhizobium* for plants.
   (d) *Rhizobium* lives on the stem of host plants.

9. Select the correct option.
The figure given below represents a plant which can ......

   (a) prepare its own food.
   (b) releases CO_2 into the soil.
   (c) derive nutrients from decaying organic matter.
   (d) suck juices from trapped insects.

10. On the basis of mode of feeding patterns, Aditya prepared four groups with three organisms in each. He added an incorrect name in one of the groups. Identify this group and select the correct option.
   (a) Mosquito, Leech and Lice
   (b) Lichen, *Rhizobium* and Mycorrhiza
   (c) Algae, *Cactus* and Rabbit
   (d) *Dionaea, Nepenthes,* Sundew

11. The most abundant gas (X) in our atmosphere cannot be utilised by plants directly in its atmospheric form. It is therefore captured by certain organisms (Y) that live symbiotically in their roots.

	Gas		Organisms
A.	Hydrogen	1.	Yeast
B.	Carbon dioxide	2.	*Rhizobium*
C.	Nitrogen	3.	Earthworm
D.	Oxygen	4.	Goats

From the table given above, mark the correct option for X and Y, respectively.

(a) A – 4 (b) B – 1 (c) C – 2 (d) D – 3

12. Refer to the diagram below showing an experimental set-up.

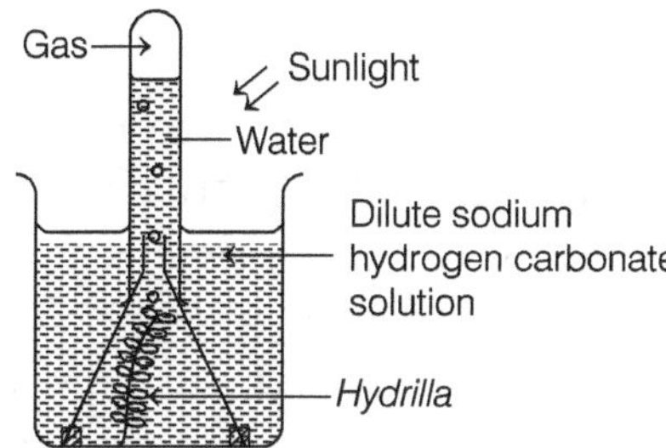

After several hours, some gas gets collected in the test tube which relights a glowing splint. Which of the following statement can be concluded from the above information?

(a) A suitable temperature is necessary for photosynthesis.
(b) Oxygen is given out during photosynthesis.
(c) Starch is produced in the aquatic plant.
(d) The gas contains carbon dioxide.

13. Preeti set up an experiment as shown in the figure. She took a destarched plant and left it in sunlight for few hours. Then, she tested X and Y leaves for the presence of starch and observed that leaf X did not respond to starch test, while leaf Y was tested positive for it.

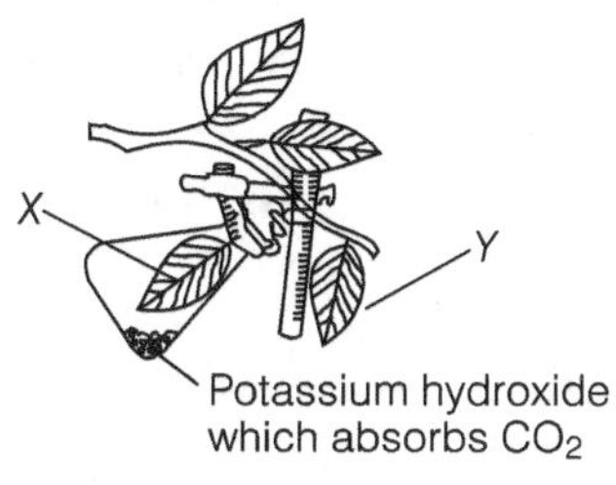

Based on this experiment, Preeti can conclude that,

(a) Chlorophyll is necessary for photosynthesis.
(b) Carbon dioxide is necessary for photosynthesis.
(c) Light is necessary for photosynthesis.
(d) Oxygen is given out during photosynthesis.

14. Refer to the diagram given below which shows an experimental set up.

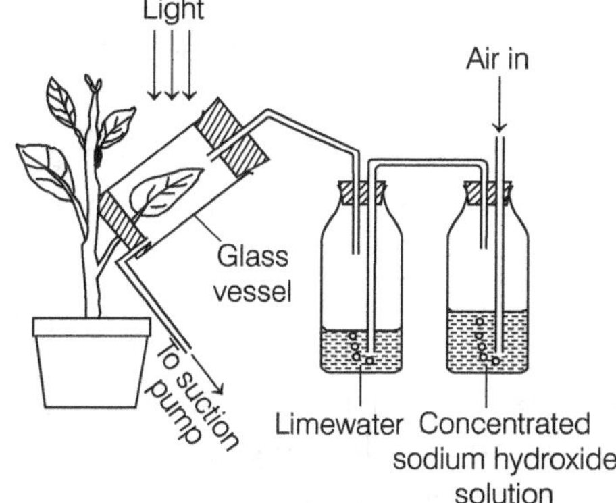

If the above experiment is successful, which of the following can probably be observed when the leaf is tested?

(a) A brick-red precipitate will be obtained with Benedict's test.
(b) A white emulsion will be obtained with ethanol emulsion test.
(c) The iodine solution will turn bluish black.
(d) The iodine solution will remain brown.

15. The teacher asked Roshan to perform an activity to test the presence of starch in leaves. Roshan wrote the steps randomly and is now confused as to how the activity is to be done?

Help him to perform the activity by arranging the steps in correct sequence.

A. Pour dilute iodine solution over leaf.

B. Boil the leaf in alcohol.

C. Pluck the green leaf from plant.

D. Wash the leaf with water to remove chlorophyll.

E. Blue-black colour.

(a) C $\longrightarrow$ A $\longrightarrow$ E $\longrightarrow$ B $\longrightarrow$ D

(b) C $\longrightarrow$ B $\longrightarrow$ E $\longrightarrow$ D $\longrightarrow$ A

(c) C $\longrightarrow$ B $\longrightarrow$ D $\longrightarrow$ A $\longrightarrow$ E

(d) E $\longrightarrow$ B $\longrightarrow$ C $\longrightarrow$ D $\longrightarrow$ A

16. What is the function of the part labelled as *A*?

Identify the plant and its mode of nutrition from the codes given below.

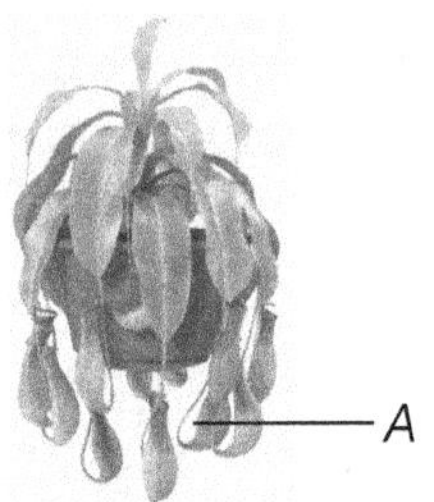

Codes

I. Flowering part of the plant

II. Trap insects for nutrition

III. Photosynthesise

IV. Pitcher plant   V. Venus flytrap

VI. Symbiotic   VII. Insectivorous

Choose the correct combination.

(a) I, V and VII   (b) II, IV and VII

(c) III, V and VII   (d) I, III and VI

2 Marks Questions

17. In the figure below, a bread that has gone bad due to growth of a microorganisms is shown. What is this organism and the method of its nutrition?

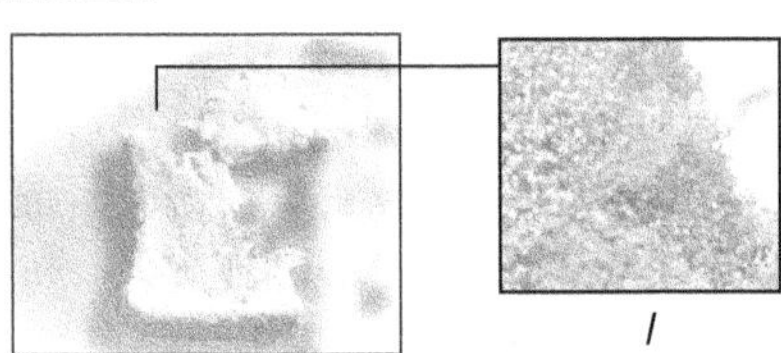

A.	Bacterial growth	1.	Parasitic
B.	Fungal growth	2.	Autotrophic
C.	Viral growth	3.	Symbiotic
D.	Lichen	4.	Saprotrophic

Choose the correct option.

(a) A – 3 (b) B – 4 (c) C – 1 (d) D – 2

18. Four test tubes as shown in the diagram below were left under sunlight for ten hours. Which of the test tubes contains the least amount of carbon dioxide?

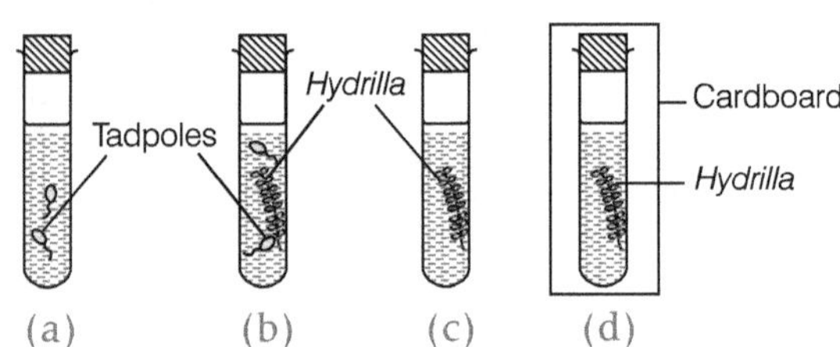

19. Refer to the figures given below.

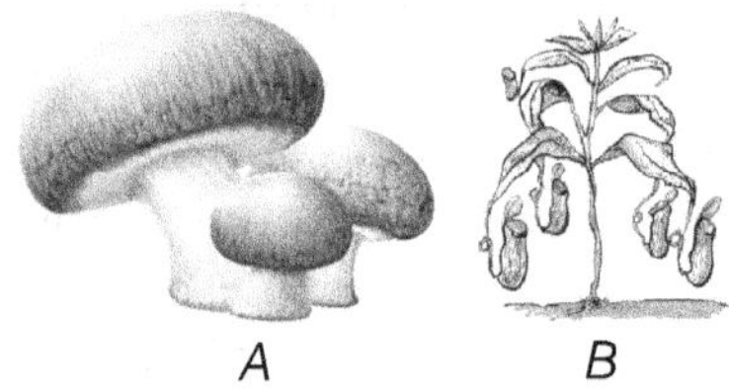

Select the statement which depicts a similarity between these two plants

(a) Both *A* and *B* have autotrophic mode of nutrition

(b) Plants *A* and *B* both lacks chlorophyll

(c) Both *A* and *B* derive nutrition from other animals

(d) Both plants reproduce through spores

20. Study the given Venn diagram.

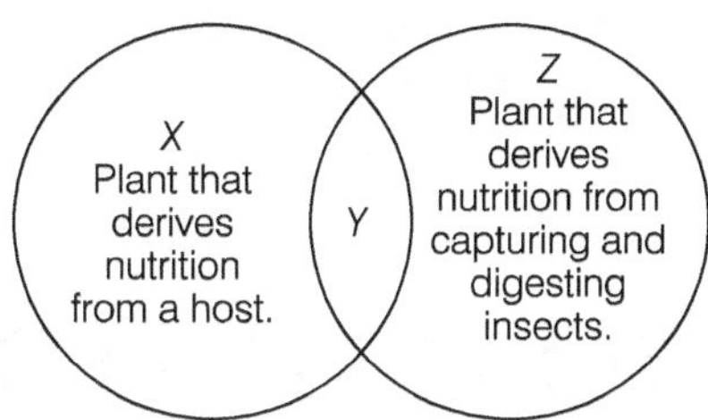

(a) Plant X could be Venus flytrap   (b) Plant Z could be *Cuscuta*
(c) Y represents heterotrophic nutrition   (d) Plant X is bread mould, plant Y is *Nepenthes*

21. Refer to the flow chart given below.

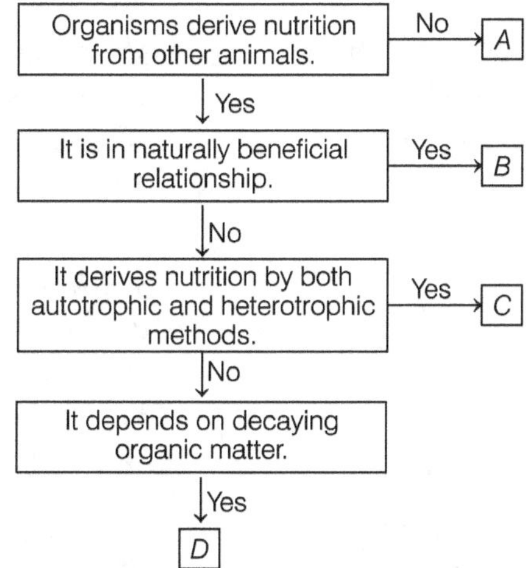

Select the option which correctly identify *A-D*.

	A	B	C	D
(a)	*Hydrilla*	Lichen	*Nepenthes*	*Rhizobium*
(b)	Wheat	Sundew	*Rhizobium*	Yeast
(c)	*Cactus*	*Rhizopus*	Lichen	*Ocimum*
(d)	Rose	*Agaricus*	*Amoeba*	Sundew

Nutrition in Animals

1 Mark Questions

1. Humans develop two sets of teeth in their lifetime. The figures below show different types of teeth. Which of these is/are used for chewing and grinding of food?

| P | Q | R | S |

   (a) Only R   (b) Only Q
   (c) Both R and S   (d) Both P and Q

2. The movement called 'peristalsis' helps in passage of food between which of the following two organs?
   (a) Rectum → Anus
   (b) Small intestine → Large intestine
   (c) Oesophagus → Stomach
   (d) Stomach → Large intestine

3. Salivary glands in mouth secrete A into the oral cavity that starts the digestion of B.
   Identify A and B.

	A	B
(a)	Bile	Fats
(b)	Amylase	Starch
(c)	Lipase	Lipids
(d)	Trypsinogen	Carbohydrate

4. Which of the following secretion of our digestive tract does not contain any digestive enzymes?
   (a) Bile   (b) Saliva
   (c) Pancreatic juice   (d) Gastric juice

5. Given below are some structures of human body. Which of the following structure is involved in the secretion of a component that breaks up fats. Also, select the component which helps in its breakdown.

A. 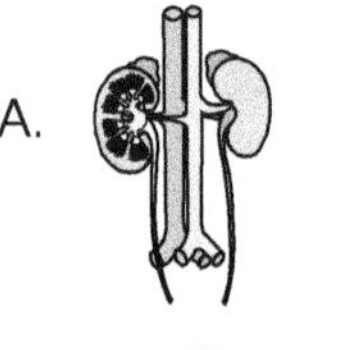   B. 

C.    D. 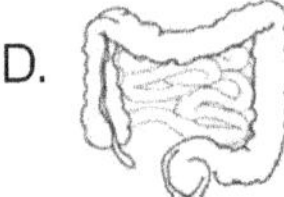

   1. Bile   2. Ptyalin   3. HCl   4. Pepsin
   Codes
   (a) A–4   (b) B–2   (c) C–1   (d) D–4

6. Which among the following actions are not involved in the process of digestion in a mammalian stomach?
   (a) Curdling of proteins in milk
   (b) Killing bacteria in food
   (c) Churning food into small pieces
   (d) Converting amino acids into urea

7. The diagram shows the human alimentary canal.

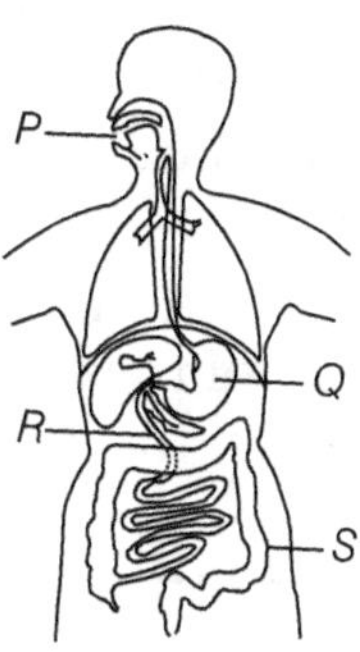

In which parts, food is digested by the action of protease?

(a) *P* and *Q*   (b) *Q* and *R*
(c) *Q* and *S*   (d) *R* and *S*

8. In the figure given below of *Amoeba* the part labelled *A* helps in intake of food, while part *B* helps in digestion of food engulfed by this organism.

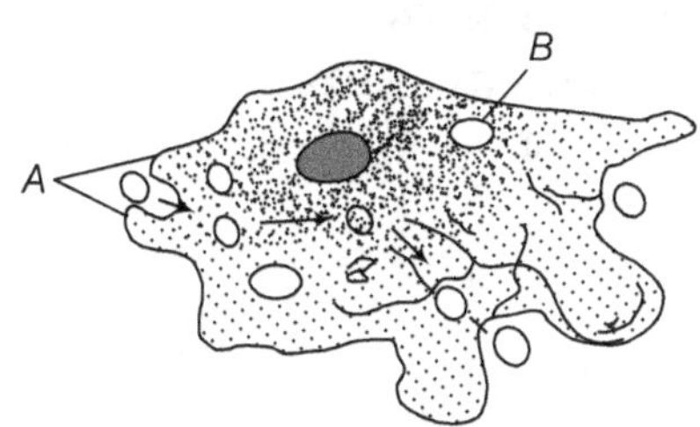

Here *A* and *B* are correctly identified as

	A	*B*
(a)	Nucleus	Cytoplasm
(b)	Food vacuole	Stomach
(c)	Ingested food	Nucleus
(d)	Pseudopodia	Food vacuole

9. Arrange the parts of digestive system below in correct order as food travels through them.

I. Gullet   II. Stomach
III. Mouth   IV. Ileum

V. Duodenum   VI. Rectum
VII. Colon   VIII. Anus

Codes
(a) III → II → I → IV → V → VI → VIII → VII
(b) II → I → III → VI → V → IV → VII → VIII
(c) III → I → II → V → IV → VII → VI → VIII
(d) I → III → II → V → IV → VII → VIII → VI

10. Read the characterstics given below.

I. Long alimentary canal.
II. Stomach with several chambers, containing anaerobic bacteria.
III. Large caecum with cellulase enzyme.
IV. Diet includes carbohydrates, fats and proteins.

Which of the following characterstics are unrelated to ruminants?

(a) Only I
(b) All except IV
(c) I and IV
(d) None of the above

11. Match the Column I with Column II.

	Column I		Column II
A.	Villi	1.	Large intestine
B.	Hydrochloric acid	2.	Liver
C.	Bile	3.	Mouth
D.	Absorption of water	4.	Stomach
E.	Mastication	5.	Small intestine

Codes

	A	B	C	D	E
(a)	1	2	3	4	5
(b)	5	4	3	2	1
(c)	5	4	2	1	3
(d)	5	4	1	2	3

12. Refer to the diagram given below which shows a section of the intestinal villus.

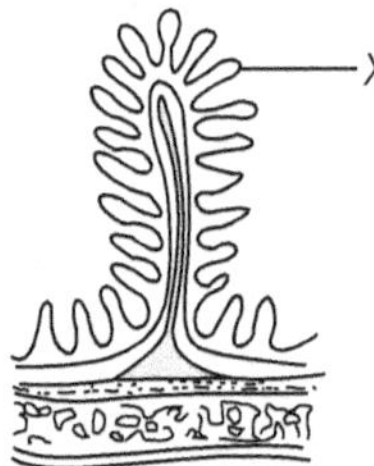

Which of the following gives a description of the cells of *X* that is correct?

(a) They have thin walls to facilitate efficient absorption.

(b) They secrete amylase to help digestion of starch.

(c) They secrete hydrochloric acid to kill bacteria.

(d) They secrete protease to help digestion of proteins.

13. Consider the given statements.

I. Small intestine is the longest part of the digestive system.

II. Minerals and vitamins do not need to be changed, they can be absorbed as such by our cells.

III. Small intestine absorbs most of water from food material.

IV. The food from duodenum goes to the lower part of the intestine, jejunum.

Which of the above statements are incorrect?

(a) I and III   (b) II and IV

(c) I and II   (d) Only III

14. The steps of the digestive process are given below in an incorrect manner.

I. Water and vitamins absorption beings.

II. Food is moistened, breakdown of proteins begins.

III. Food mixes with amylase.

IV. Proteins, carbohydrates and fats breakdown and nutrients are absorbed into the bloodstream.

Select the option that gives the correct order of these events as food passes through the human digestive tract.

(a) II, IV, I and III   (b) IV, II , III and I

(c) I, III, II and IV   (d) III, II, IV and I

15. State [T] for True or [F] for False.

I. Energy value of food is measured in calories.

II. The semi-digested food is called chyle.

III. Cellulose (a derivative of carbohydrate) can be digested in our digestive system.

IV. In the absence of peristalsis, food cannot travel down the oesophagus.

Codes

	I	II	III	IV
(a)	T	F	T	F
(b)	F	T	F	T
(c)	T	T	F	F
(d)	F	F	F	T

16. In the figure below, a cow that eats grass is shown. A component of grass is digestible in its stomach but not in humans due to part labelled as *X*.

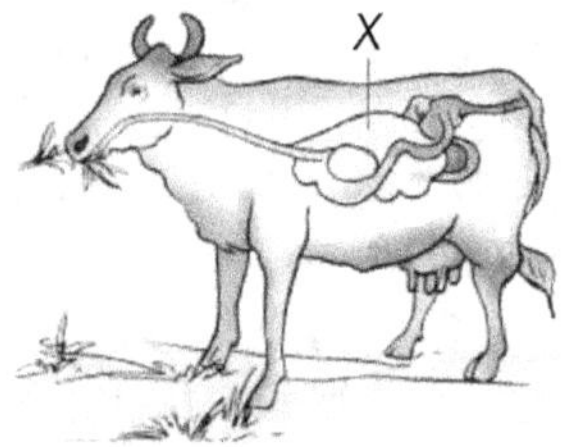

Identify X and select the correct regarding it

(a) X is the chamber where 'cud' is stored temporarily.
(b) X is the true stomach in ruminants.
(c) X is rumen where anaerobic bacteria helps in digestion of cellulose.
(d) X is the chamber where proteins are digested by specific enzyme.

17. State [T] for True or [F] for False.
   I. Fat is completely digested in small intestine.
   II. Our small intestine is approximately 20-25 inches long.
   III. Nutrients are removed from the undigested food when it is in the large intestine.
   IV. Digestion process begins in the stomach part of the human digestive system.
   V. The gall bladder temporarily stores bile.

Codes

	I	II	III	IV	V
(a)	T	T	T	F	T
(b)	T	T	F	T	T
(c)	T	F	T	T	T
(d)	T	F	F	T	F

2 Marks Questions

18. The experimental apparatus shows the action of saliva on starch.

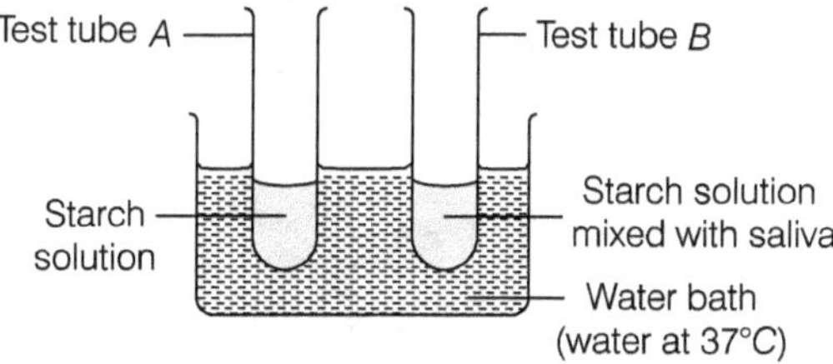

The temperature of the water bath kept at 37°C and not at room temperature because
(a) the human body temperature is 37°C.
(b) enzyme work fastly at 37°C.
(c) starch dissolve properly at 37°C.
(d) it is difficult to maintain water temperature at room temperature with enzyme.

19. Given below are reactions that takes place in

   I. Stomach
   $$X \xrightarrow{\text{Pepsin}} \text{Peptones}$$

   II. Small intestine
   $$\text{Starch} \xrightarrow{Y} \text{Maltose}$$

   III. Small intestine
   $$\text{Fats} \xrightarrow{\text{Bile}} Z$$

In these reactions, X, Y and Z are
(a) Starch, pepsin, peptides and peptones
(b) Proteins, pancreatic amylase, fatty acids and glycerol
(c) Fats, salivary amylase, sugars
(d) Dietary fibres, trypsin, peptides and peptones

20. Small samples I, II, III of digestive juices from parts X, Y and Z of a human alimentary canal were collected. A drop of each sample was placed on a thin strip coated with protein as shown below

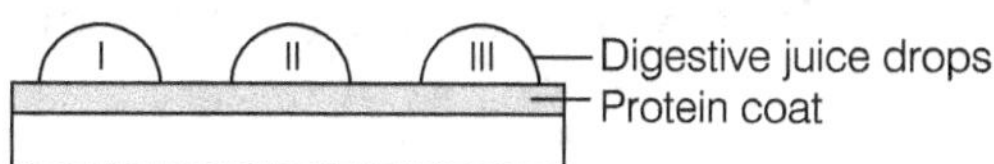

After some time, it was observed that the protein coat was digested completely by enzyme II and partially by enzyme III.

Choose the option that correctly identifies the site X, Y and Z of alimentary canal from where the samples were collected.

	X	Y	Z
(a)	Stomach	Liver	Mouth
(b)	Mouth	Large intestine	Stomach
(c)	Small intestine	Mouth	Liver
(d)	Mouth	Small intestine	Stomach

21. The diagram below shows part of the digestive system, liver, pancreas and associated blood vessels. Which labelled structure will carry the highest concentration of dissolved amino acids in them?

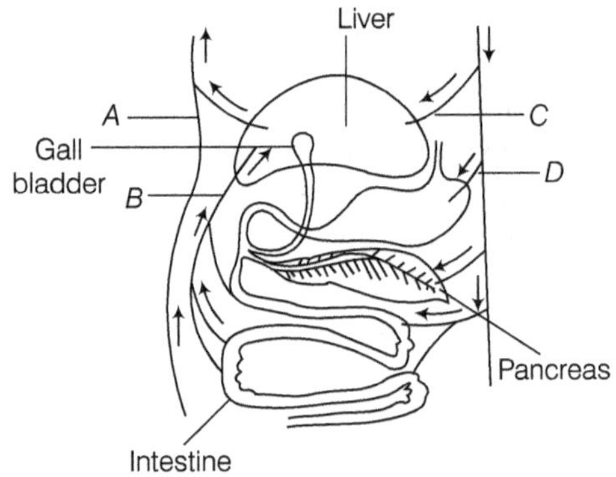

(a) D (b) C
(c) B (d) A

22. Given below is a picture of human tongue with parts labelled I-IV, identifying the points which helps us to identify different tastes.

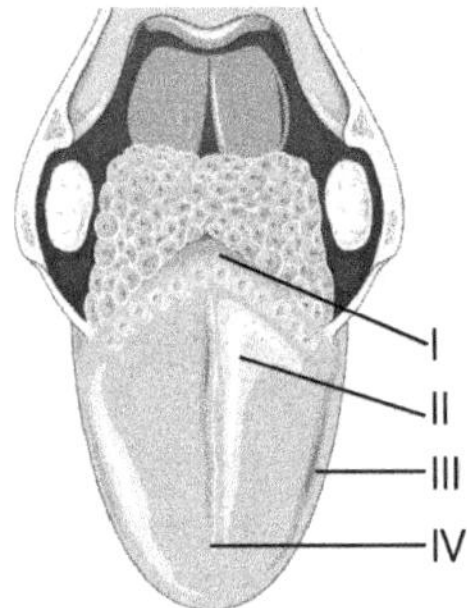

Which labelled part of the tongue will help in confirming that food we just tasted is sour?
(a) II   (b) IV
(c) I   (d) III

23. Refer to the given figure of a part of human digestive system and select the correct option regarding the labelled parts X, Y and Z.

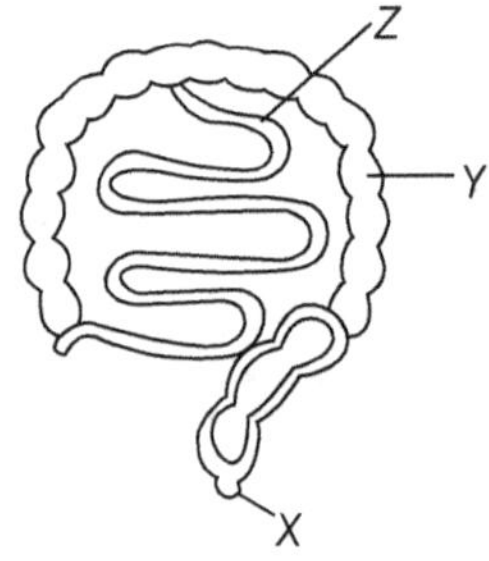

(a) Y absorbs water and some salts from the undigestable food matter.
(b) Food is completely absorbed in part X of the alimentary canal.
(c) X secretes bile juice whereas Y secretes hydrochloric acid.
(d) X absorbs water from undigestable remains, while Z secretes digestive enzymes *viz*, amylase, lipase, etc.

Fibre to Fabric

1 Mark Questions

1. Larvae of silkworm feed on
(a) bamboo leaves   (b) mulberry leaves
(c) banyan leaves   (d) neem leaves

2. The process of rearing of silkworm to obtain silk is called
(a) apiculture   (b) sericulture
(c) pisciculture   (d) floriculture

3. The fibre obtained from silkworm is a
(a) protein   (b) carbohydrate
(c) keratin   (d) cellulose

4. The figure given below shows a stage of life cycle of silk moth. Identify which stage is this.

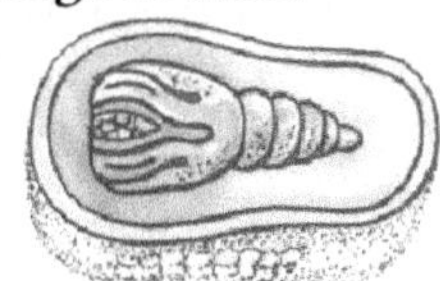

(a) Eggs on mulberry
(b) Cocoon
(c) Cocoon with developing moth
(d) Pupa developing to silk adult moth

5. How many eggs a female silk moth lay?
(a) 15 to 20   (b) 300 to 400
(c) 3000 to 5000   (d) 1 or 2

6. At which stage silkworm produces silk?
(a) Egg   (b) Larval   (c) Pupa   (d) Cocoon

7. Two groups of fibre are given below that are used to make dresses.
Group I Jute, Cotton
Group II Silk, Wool
Find the correct statement for each group.
(a) Group I is natural fibre whereas, Group II is synthetic fibres.
(b) Group I are obtain from part of plant and Group II are obtain from animals.
(c) Group I is found in humid climate whereas Group II are found in dry, hot climatic condition.
(d) Both (a) and (b) are correct

8. Find the odd one out.
(a) Lohi   (b) Changthangi
(c) Marwari   (d) Nali

9. Yak wool is commonly found in which of the following place?
(a) Jammu and Kashmir
(b) Tibet and Ladakh
(c) South America
(d) Himachal Pradesh and Uttarakhand

10. Which of the following disease is common in workers working in wool industry?
(a) Dermatitis   (b) Musculoskeleton
(c) Sorter's disease   (d) Asbestos

11. By which method the dust, dirt and grease is removed from the fleece?
  (a) Reeling   (b) Shearing
  (c) Scouring   (d) Rolling

12. Which of the following is the correct sequence of dyeing process?
  (a) Shearing → Scouring → Sorting → Dyeing → Straightening
  (b) Scouring → Shearing → Sorting → Straightening → Dyeing
  (c) Sorting → Shearing → Scouring → Straightening → Dyeing
  (d) Straightening → Shearing → Sorting → Scouring → Dyeing

13. Indentify the correct relation

  Alpca : Breed of camel : : _______ : Breed of goat
  (a) Llama   (b) Baluchi
  (c) Angora   (d) Bannur

14. The wool of which Indian breed of sheep is used to make woolen shawls?
  (a) Nali   (b) Marwari
  (c) Patanwadi   (d) Bakharwal

15. Read the following statements and identify the incorrect statement.
  I. The process of shearing hurts the sheep.
  II. Reeling is the process of unwinding the silk fibre from cocoon.
  Codes
  (a) Only statement I is incorrect
  (b) Only statement II is incorrect
  (c) Both statements I and II are incorrect
  (d) Both statements I and II are correct

16. Some variety of animal fibres are given below. Select the option in which all the variety is obtain of same animal.
  (a) Llama, Merino, Mohair
  (b) Shettand, Cashmere, Angora
  (c) Mulberry, Tassar, Muga
  (d) Merino, Cashmere, Angora

17. State [T] for True and [F] for False.
  I. Silk is the strongest natural fibre.
  II. Rearing of sheep help them to survive in hot weather.
  III. Fleece of an animal act as an insulating covering, which protect them from cold weather.
  IV. Pashmina shawl is obtained from cashmere sheep.
  Codes

	I	II	III	IV		I	II	III	IV
(a)	T	F	F	F	(b)	T	T	F	T
(c)	F	F	T	T	(d)	T	F	T	F

18. Which of the following is incorrect?
  (a) Cotton clothes are light and absorb moisture.
  (b) Woolen clothes trap the air between fibres hence, keep us worm.
  (c) Cotton clothes should not be wear, while working in kitchen as they easily catch fire.
  (d) Wool can undergo biodegradation.

19. Match the Column I with Column II.

	Column I		Column II
A.	Marwari	1.	Carpet wool
B.	Patanwadi	2.	Brown fleece
C.	Rampur Bushair	3.	Gujarat
D.	Nali	4.	Coarse wool
		5.	Jammu and Kashmir

  Codes

	A	B	C	D
(a)	4	2	5	2
(b)	5	2	4	1
(c)	4	3	2	1
(d)	2	3	1	4

20. Consider the given term below and choose the correct statement for them.

I. Weaving　　II. Knitting

(a) Process-I is done by using single strand of yarn whereas process-II is done by using two strand of yarn.

(b) Both the process are done by two strand of yarn, but in weaving two different colour of yarn is used.

(c) Process-I is done by using two strand of yarn whereas process-II is done by using single strand of yarn.

(d) Both is done by using single strand of yarn.

2 Marks Questions

21. Observe the cyclic representation given below of silk formation. The option that correctly declares the time of each phase of the cycle.

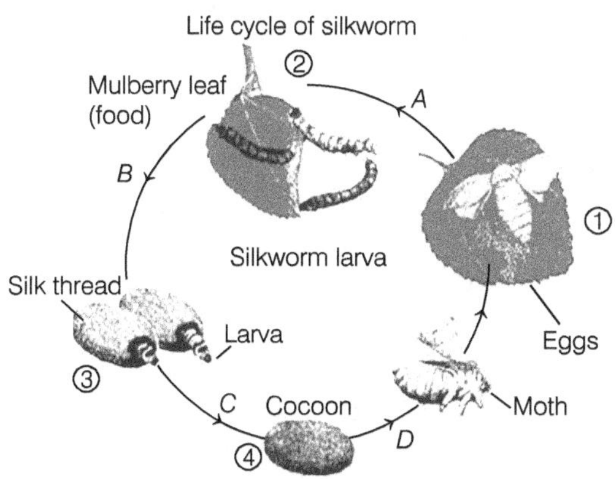

Codes

	A	B	C	D
(a)	10 days	4-6 weeks	3-8 days	16 days
(b)	16 days	3-8 days	4-6 weeks	10 days
(c)	10 days	3-8 days	4-6 weeks	16 days
(d)	3-8 days	4-6 weeks	16 days	10 days

22. Read the given statements carefully and identify the correct option regarding P, Q, R and S.

P-It is known as the most superior quality of silk.

Q-This is used to separate different textures of fibres according to its quality.

R-Silk is mainly made up of this protein.

S-It is the process in which sheared skin with hair is washed to remove grease and dust.

Choose the correct option.

	P	Q	R	S
(a)	Eri silk	Grading	Fibroin	Carding
(b)	Tasar silk	Sorting	Keratin	Carding
(c)	Mulberry silk	Sorting	Keratin	Scouring
(d)	Mulberry silk	Grading	Fibroin	Scouring

23. Refer to the given figure P, Q and R below

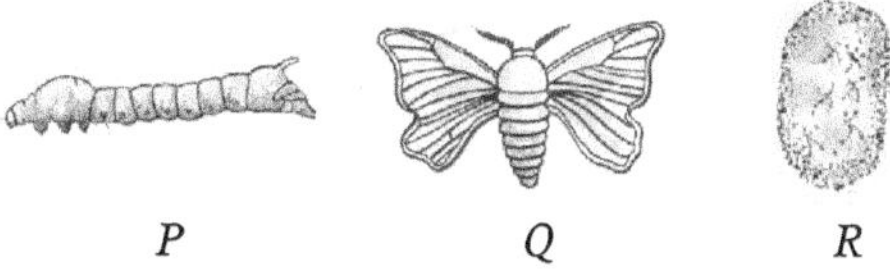

Some statements are made by four students. Identify who made the incorrect statement?

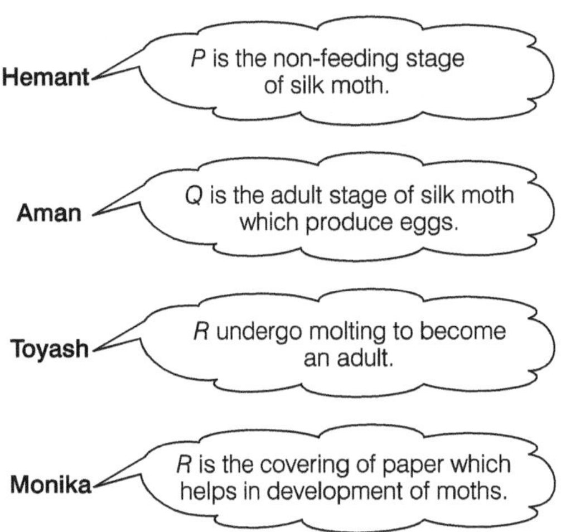

(a) Hemant and Monika
(b) Aman and Toyash
(c) Monika and Aman
(d) Hemant and Toyash

24. Raman and Anshu want to identify fibre X and Y, they burn both the fibre and note some observation.

		X	Y
1.	On burning	Burn slowly	Burn with yellow flame
2.	Smell on burning	Smells of charred meat	Smell of burnt paper
3.	Burnt reside	Ash	Ash

Choose the correct statement regarding X and Y.

(a) Fibre X is the strongest natural fibre, whereas fibre Y is the most important cash crop in India.
(b) Fibre X is strong and extremly absorbent, whereas Y is weak and produce luxurious fabrics.
(c) Fibre X is long, rough and shiny fibre, whereas Y is strong and resistant to crease.
(d) Fibre X produce, solf, thick and wrinkle resistant fabric, whereas Y produces soft, comfortable and lustrous fabric.

25. Refer to the given flow chart.

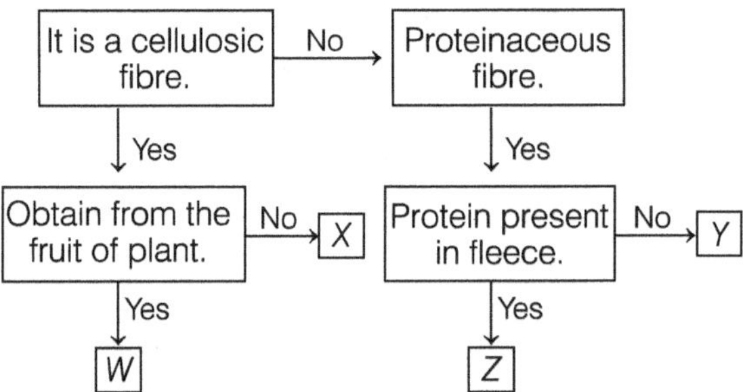

Select the correct statement regarding W, X, Y and Z.

(a) X-is obtain from the leave of plant, Z- is obtain by rearing of animal.
(b) W-is grown in black soil, Y-is found in hilly areas.
(c) Z-is made up of protein called keratin, Y-is made up of fibroin protein.
(d) X-is obtain from stem of plant, Y-is called golden fibre.

Chapter 04

Heat

1 Mark Questions

1. Which of the following is not a measuring unit of temperature?
   (a) Kelvin   (b) Joule
   (c) Celsius   (d) Fahrenheit

2. What is the direction of heat flow in the diagram below?

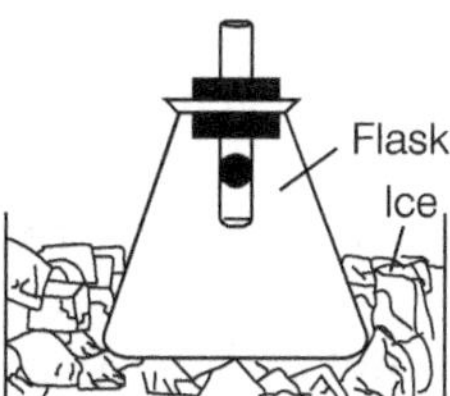

   (a) From the flask to the ice
   (b) From the ice to the flask
   (c) From the surroundings to the air trapped inside
   (d) From the ice to the surroundings

3. The body of thermos is usually made up of metal to keep the beverages hot for longer period of time. Why do the outer cover and lid of thermos is made up of plastic?
   (a) To prevent loss of heat by conduction
   (b) To prevent loss of heat by convection
   (c) To increase the durability of thermos
   (d) To prevent loss of heat by radiation

4. Paheli after pouring hot tea in a cup covers it with a plate. How does covering a cup of hot tea reduce the heat loss by the tea?

   (a) The cover is a poor radiator of heat
   (b) The cover greatly reduces heat loss by radiation
   (c) The cover greatly reduces heat loss by conduction
   (d) The cover minimises the formation of convection currents above the tea

5. Which of the following diagrams shows correctly the convection currents of air in a closed beaker when heated?

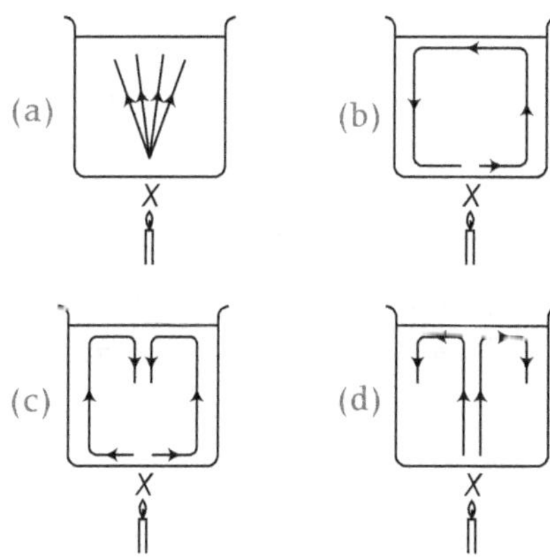

6. In liquids, thermal energy is transferred mainly by convection. What is the cause of convection?
   (a) Change in temperature
   (b) Change in density
   (c) Infrared radiation
   (d) Expansion

7. A student heated a large beaker filled with water on a bunsen burner.

Which of the following options would describe the correct process on the points X, Y and Z ?

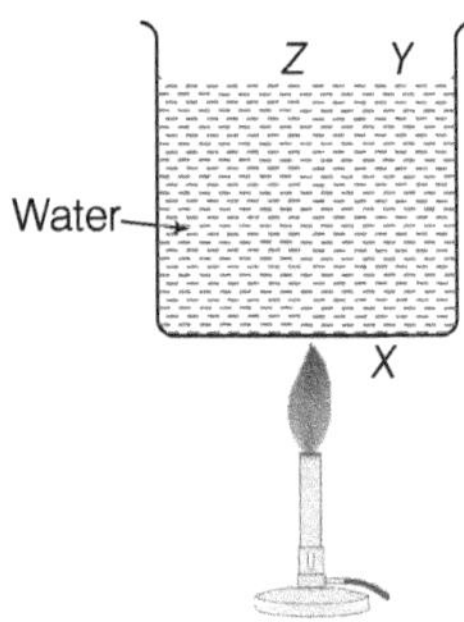

(a) Cooling at X
(b) Cooling at Y
(c) Heating at Y
(d) Heating at Z

8. The term thermal equilibrium refers to the stage when
(a) two liquids are at same temperature
(b) all the liquids are at same temperature
(c) all the objects involved and the surroundings are at same temperature
(d) conduction, convection and radiation all occur simultaneously

9. Some drops of wax are stuck to the wooden rod as shown in the figure below

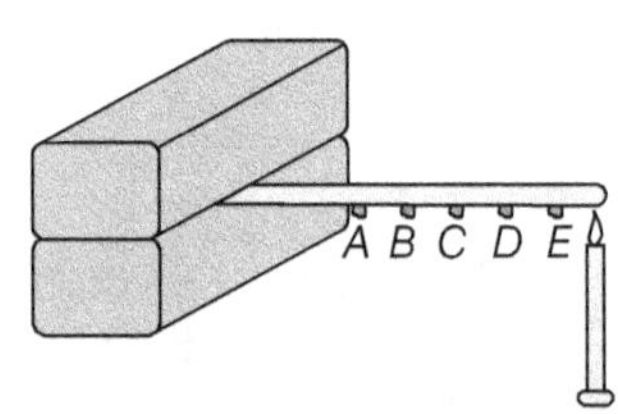

Which of them will melt first?
(a) E (b) A
(c) C (d) None of these

10. What is the reason behind having some space between the successive lines of railway tracks?

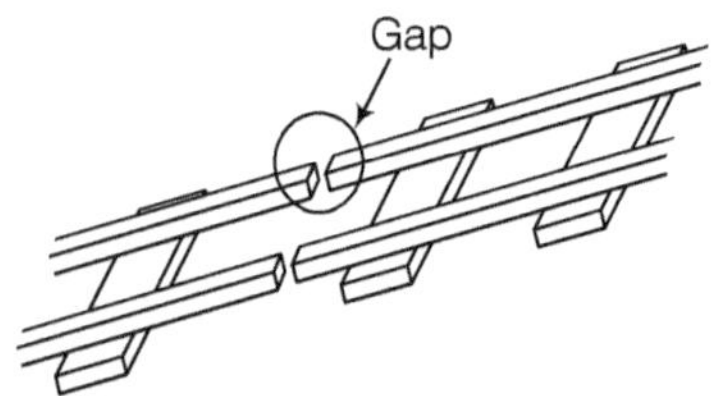

(a) To allow trains to go smoothly
(b) To allow the flow of electricity
(c) To allow expansion of tracks in summer and contraction in winters
(d) To allow contraction of tracks in summer and expansion in winters

11. Fuel is usually transported in tanks with shiny or white surfaces. Which of the following gives the best explanation for the above?
(a) To increase visibility and prevent accidents
(b) To reflect the heat from the Sun and prevent ignition of the fuel
(c) To allow the tank to lose heat quickly
(d) To keep the fuel in the tank warm

12. A clinical thermometer shows a patient's body temperature even after it has been taken out from his mouth. This is because
(a) the capillary tube has a very narrow bore
(b) it has a constriction near the bulb
(c) the density of mercury is very high
(d) the stem of the thermometer contracts

13. Aril wanted to have a drink of milk but found it too hot to drink. He then placed it in a container of cold water.

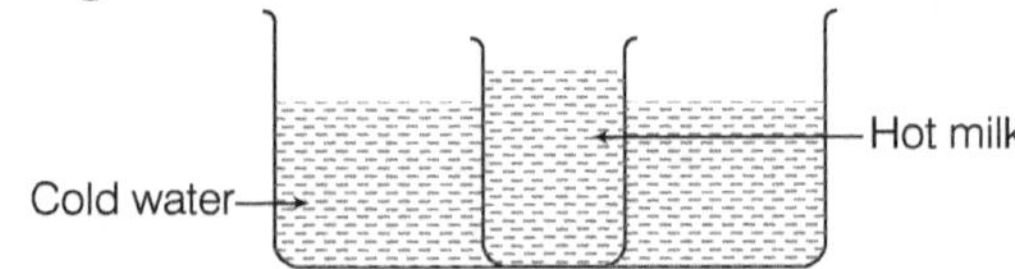

After a while ....
(a) the hot milk gained coldness from the cold water and became cooler
(b) the temperature of the hot milk decreases to become lower than the cold water
(c) the temperature of the cold water decreases as it loses heat to the hot milk
(d) the temperature of the cold water rises as it gains heat from the hot milk

14. Four arrangements to measure temperature of ice in beaker with laboratory thermometer are shown in figures given below. Which one of them shows the correct arrangement for accurate measurement of temperature?

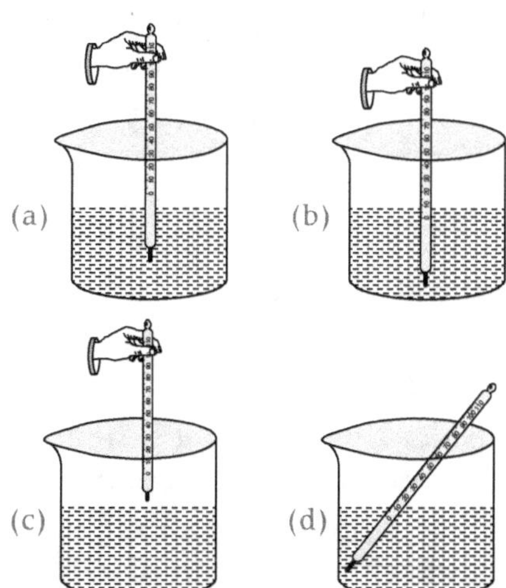

15. A clinical thermometer is designed to respond quickly to a change in temperature and to have a high sensitivity.

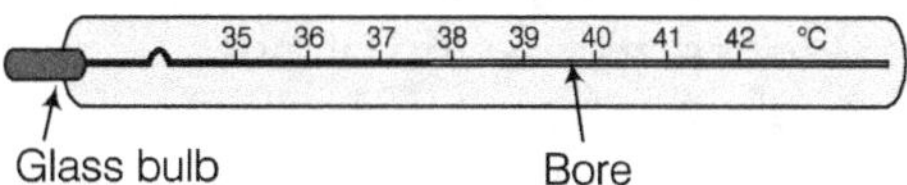

Which design feature should the clinical thermometer have?

	Bulb	Bore
(a)	Thick glass	narrow
(b)	Thick glass	wide
(c)	Thin glass	narrow
(d)	Thin glass	wide

16. Tina ordered a plate of fish and chips. When her meal arrived, it was piping hot. She cut it into small bite-sized pieces and after a while, she found that she was able to eat them without burning her tongue. Why was this so?
(a) Heat from the food is lost to the surroundings
(b) The air from the surroundings warms the food
(c) The temperature of the food falls because there was wind
(d) The food gained heat from the surroundings causing the temperature to rise

17. Boojho has three thermometers as shown in the given figure. He wants to measure the temperature of his body and that of boiling water. Which thermometer(s) should he choose?

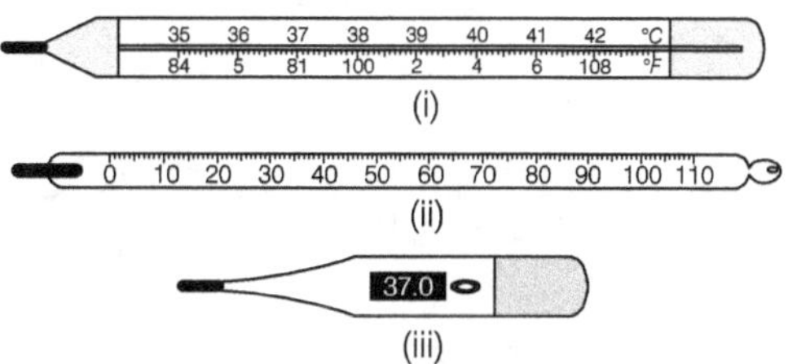

(a) Thermometer (i) or (iii) for measuring the temperature of body and (ii) for measuring the temperature of boiling water
(b) Thermometer (i) for measuring temperature of both
(c) Thermometer (ii) for measuring temperature of both
(d) Thermometer (iii) for measuring temperature of both

18. Two thermometers *A* and *B* are placed in sunshine for equal time. The bulb of *A* is coated with lamp black while the bulb of *B* is coated with silver. Which of them will show a higher rise in thermometer?

(a) *A*

(b) *B*

(c) Both (a) and (b) will rise equally

(d) Neither of them will rise

19. Radha bakes cake in the oven, what happens to the baked cake when she takes it out from the oven

(a) It gains heat from the surroundings and cools down

(b) It loses heat to the surroundings and cools down

(c) It gains heat from the surroundings and maintains its temperature

(d) It loses heat to the surroundings and maintains its temperature

20. Figures show a student reading a doctor's thermometer. Which of the figure indicates the correct method of reading temperature?

(a)    (b) 

(c) 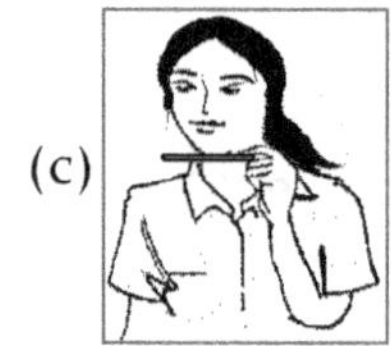   (d) None of these

21. Consider the following statements and choose the correct ones.

I. The level of expansion of mercury is used to measure the temperature of a substance using a thermometer.

II. The normal temperature of a human is the average body temperature of a large number of healthy persons.

III. Clinical thermometer measures temperature more accurately than laboratory thermometer.

Codes

(a) I and II

(b) II and III

(c) I and III

(d) All of the above

22. Consider the following statements and choose the correct ones.

I. The kink present in laboratory thermometer helps to measure the temperature of a room.

II. The kink is a sharp bent in the capillary of a thermometer.

III. The range of laboratory thermometer is $-10°C$ to $110°C$.

Codes

(a) I and II

(b) II and III

(c) I and III

(d) All of the above

23. Consider the following statements and choose the incorrect one.

I. Conduction needs a material medium for transmission of heat.

II. Conduction and convection need a material medium for transmission of heat.

III. Conduction, convection and radiation need a material medium for transmission of heat.

Codes

(a) Both I and III

(b) Only I

(c) Only II

(d) Only III

24. Consider the following statements and choose the correct one using the codes given below.

I. Wool is a good conductor of heat due to which it allows outside heat to enter into our body and keep us warm.

II. The air trapped in fibres of woollen clothes, stops the flow of heat from our body to cold surroundings.

III. Water transfers heat by the process of conduction.

Codes
(a) Only I
(b) Only II
(c) Only III
(d) None of the above

25. Dinesh set up the experiment as shown below:

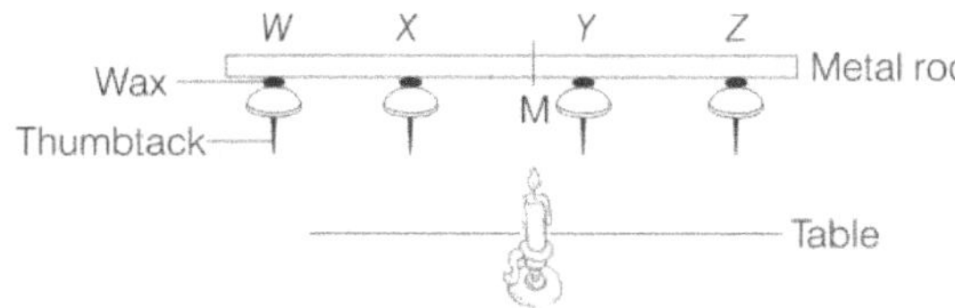

He placed the lighted candle below the metal rod at position M. He used the same amount of wax to hold all the thumbtacks at W, X, Y and Z on the rod. Arrange the thumbtacks according to the time each of them takes to drop from the rod, from the first to the last.
(a) Y, X, W, Z
(b) X, Y, W, Z
(c) Y, X, Z, W
(d) W, Z, Y, X

26. Yuvraj and Rohit are on a camping trip and they are sleeping outdoors without a tent. Yuvraj covered himself with one thick blanket whereas Rohit used two thin blankets. In the middle of the night, Yuvraj had trouble sleeping as he was feeling cold but Rohit managed to stay warm and slept well. Which of the following statements explains why two thin blankets are better than one thick blanket for warmth?
(a) The thick blanket trapped more air than the thin blankets causing the air to move freely around Yuvraj making him cold
(b) Air trapped in between the two thin blankets prevented the heat from Rohit's body from escaping and kept him warm
(c) Thick materials conduct heat more than thin materials
(d) Thin materials are better insulators than thick materials

2 Marks Questions

27. Mark where the heat is being transferred by conduction, convection and radiation.

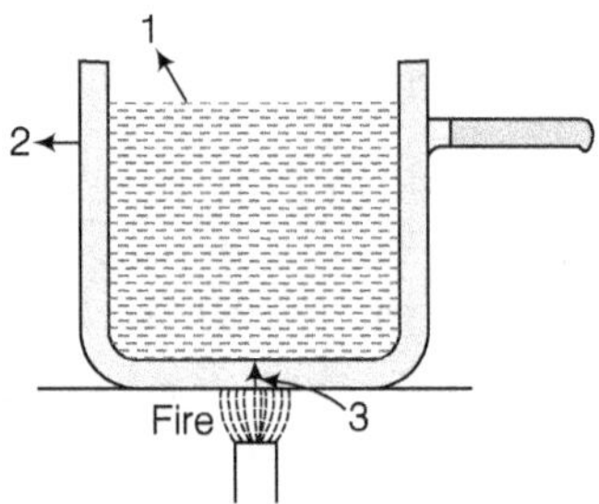

(a) 1-conduction, 2-convection, 3-radiation
(b) 1-convection, 2-radiation, 3-conduction
(c) 1-radiation, 2-conduction, 3-convection
(d) 1-radiation, 2-convection, 3-conduction

28. The diagram shows a crystal being heated in a beaker of water. The crystal releases a dye which shows how the water circulates around the beaker.

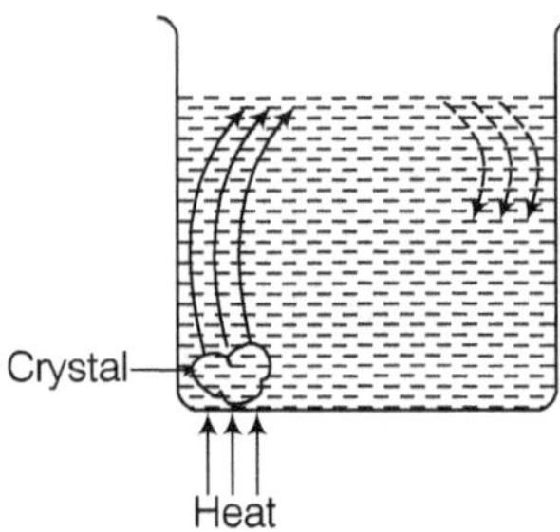

What is happening to cause the water above the crystal to rise?

(a) The water contracts and its density decreases
(b) The water contracts and its density increases
(c) The water expands and its density decreases
(d) The water expands and its density increases

29. The diagram below shows two thermometers, *P* and *Q* placed near a Bunsen flame.

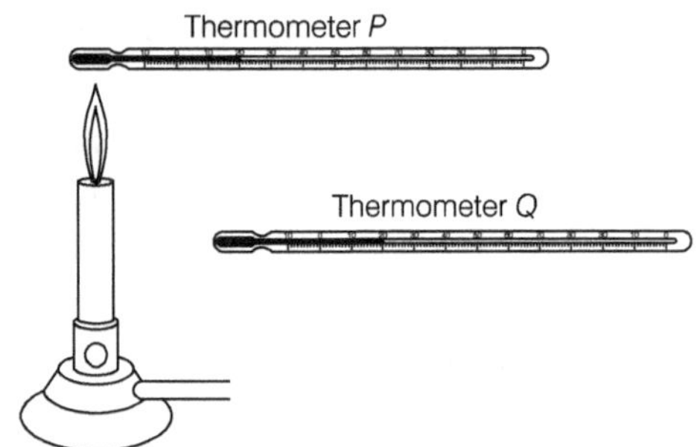

Which of the following pairs of processes correctly describe how the two thermometers got heated up by the Bunsen flame?

	Thermometer *P*	**Thermometer *Q***
(a)	Radiation	Radiation
(b)	Radiation, conduction	Convection
(c)	Convection	Radiation
(d)	Radiation, convection	Radiation

30. Match the given matrix.

A.	Temperature	1.	35°C to 42°C
B.	Clinical thermometer	2.	No mercury
C.	Laboratory thermometer	3.	Weather forecasting
D.	Digital thermometer	4.	Degree of hotness
E.	Maximum-minimum thermometer	5.	−10°C to 110°C

Codes

	A	B	C	D	E
(a)	4	5	1	2	3
(b)	4	1	5	2	3
(c)	4	5	1	3	2
(d)	3	1	5	2	4

Chapter 05

Acids, Bases and Salts

1 Mark Questions

1. Acids present in spinach, amla and unripen grapes respectively are
(a) tartaric acid, oxalic acid, citric acid
(b) oxalic acid, ascorbic acid, tartaric acid
(c) tartaric acid, citric acid, oxalic acid
(d) ascorbic acid, oxalic acid, tartaric acid

2. Complete the following sentences by choosing appropriate set of words for (i) to (iv).
I. The sour things we eat contain ..(i).....
II. Ammonium hydroxide is ....(ii)....
III. An acid is called .... (iii)... acid if obtained from animals or plants.
IV. An antacid generally contains a ...(iv)....

Codes

	(i)	(ii)	(iii)	(iv)
(a)	acid	acid	strong	base
(b)	acid	base	weak	alkali
(c)	acid	base	organic	base
(d)	base	acid	mineral	base

3. Shikha classified some of the household items present around her into acids and bases.

	Acids		Bases
1.	Orange	4.	Washing soda
2.	Antacid	5.	Baking soda
3.	Tea	6.	Curd

Which of them is/are placed under the wrong category?
(a) 1 and 6   (b) 2 and 5
(c) 2 and 6   (d) 3 and 4

4. The dilute solutions of which of the following are not harmful to drink?
I. Magnesium hydroxide
II. Potassium hydroxide
III. Sodium hydrogen carbonate
IV. Sodium carbonate

Codes
(a) I and II   (b) II and III
(c) I and III   (d) II and IV

5. Some acids alongwith their sources are as follows:

	Acids	Sources	
		Natural	**Mineral**
1.	Lactic	✗	✓
2.	Carbonic	✓	✗
3.	Tartaric	✓	✗
4.	Sulphuric	✗	✓

Key: ✓ Yes
       × No

The correct match(es) is/are
(a) Only 1   (b) Only 3
(c) 3 and 4   (d) 2 and 4

6. Some bases alongwith their sources are given below. Which of these matchings is incorrect?

	Base	Source
(a)	Calcium hydroxide	Lime water
(b)	Ammonium hydroxide	Window cleaner
(c)	Magnesium hydroxide	Whitewash
(d)	Potassium hydroxide	Soap

7. Ravi found that the turmeric stain on his shirt turned red when his mother washed it with soap, but he was unable to understand the cause of this change. What do you think is the reason for this?

I. Turmeric is acidic in nature.

II. The soap solution is acidic.

III. Turmeric is a natural indicator.

IV. The soap solution is basic.

Codes

(a) I and II   (b) I and III

(c) II and III   (d) III and IV

8. **Statement I** Blue vitriol turns blue litmus red.

Statement II Aqueous solution of blue vitriol is acidic.

Choose the correct option.

(a) Only statement I is correct

(b) Only statement II is correct

(c) Both statements are correct

(d) Both statements are incorrect

9. Rama performed the following three experiments by using vinegar solution.

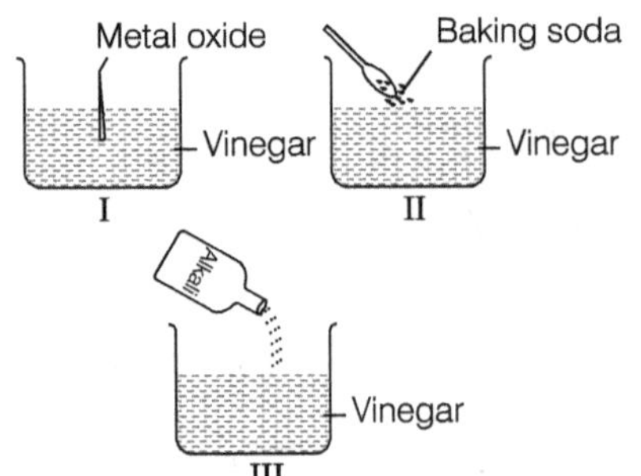

What common product she got in the above three experiments?

(a) Water   (b) Hydrogen

(c) Salt   (d) Carbon dioxide

10. Which of the following test(s) will successfully prove that an unknown substance X is an acid? Substance X is known to have the ability to remove rust from metal surfaces.

I. Litmus test

II. pH meter

III. React X with carbonates

IV. React X with magnesium ribbon

Codes

(a) Only II   (b) I and III

(c) II, III and IV   (d) All of these

11. Consider the following two types of containers.

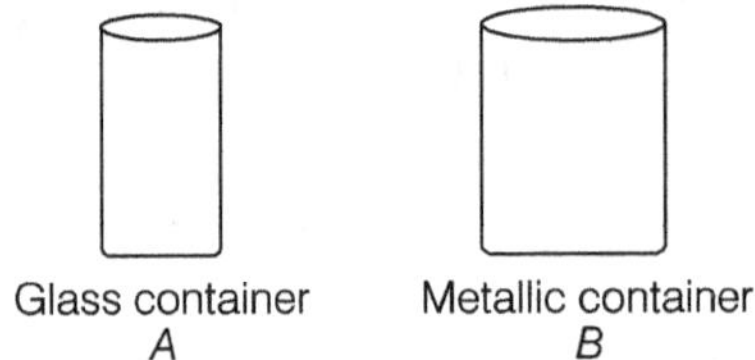

Rama preferred A for storing cut pieces of lemon. This is because

I. A is transparent.   II. A is cheaper.

III. B is not easily available.

IV. B reacts with the acid present in lemon.

The correct reason(s) is/are

(a) I and III   (b) II and IV

(c) I and II   (d) Only IV

12. One day Reeta went to jeweller's shop with her mother. Her mother gave an old gold jewellery to the goldsmith to polish. Next day, when they brought the jewellery back, they found that there was a slight loss in its weight. Goldsmith had dissolved the jewellery in solution X. Here X is

(a) phosphoric acid   (b) sulphuric acid

(c) nitric acid   (d) *aqua-regia*

13. Some of the substances are given below.

    I. Red cabbage   II. Turmeric
   III. Litmus paper   IV. Aspirin
    V. Phenolphthalein   VI. Vinegar
  VII. Milk of magnesia
 VIII. Aerated drinks

In which pair, both are the indicators?
(a) I and II   (b) III and IV
(c) V and VI   (d) VI and VIII

14. Consider the following statements.

Statement I Their taste is sour.

Statement II When concentrated, they are corrosive in nature.

Statement III Their strength is measured in terms of hydrogen ion concentration.

Which of these is/are true for both acids and bases?
(a) I and II   (b) I and III
(c) II and III   (d) I, II and III

15. Consider the following flow chart.

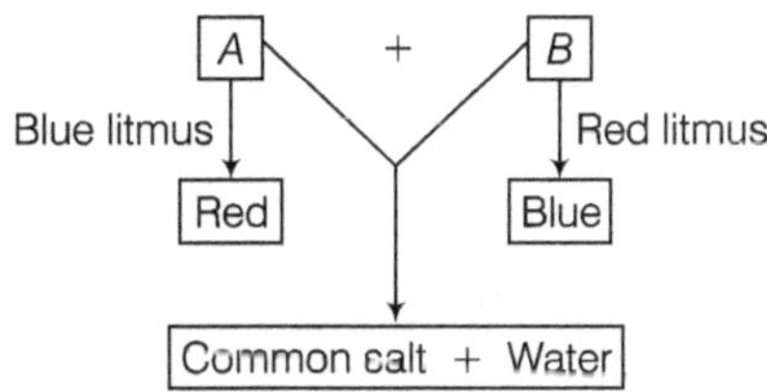

A and *B* are
(a) $A = NaOH$, $B = NaCl$
(b) $A = HCl$, $B = NaOH$
(c) $A = NaOH$, $B = HCl$
(d) $A = HCl$, $B = H_2O$

16. If a few drops of a concentrated acid accidently spill over the hand of a student, what should be done?
(a) Wash the hand with saline solution
(b) Wash the hand immediately with plenty of water and apply a paste of sodium hydrogen carbonate
(c) After washing with plenty of water apply solution of sodium hydroxide on the hand
(d) Neutralise the acid with a strong alkali

17. **Statement I** Solution of common salt is acidic.

Statement II Solution of common salt turns blue litmus blue.

Choose the correct option.
(a) Only statement I is correct.
(b) Only statement II is correct.
(c) Both statements are correct.
(d) Both statements are incorrect.

18. Sodium chloride (common salt) is an important component of our diet and is formed by the reaction between
(a) dichlorine and sodium hydride
(b) hydrochloric acid and sodium hydride
(c) hydrochloric acid and sodium hydroxide
(d) dichlorine and sodium hydroxide

19. Two farmers *A* and *B* found a sharp decrease in their crop yield. *A* observed that it is because of the sprinkling of excessive fertilisers while *B* found a supply of washing run off of clothes to his field. Could you suggest what they should add to regain high yield of crops?
(a) *A* : Organic matter *B* : Quicklime
(b) *A* : Quicklime *B* : Organic matter
(c) *A* and *B* : Quicklime
(d) *A* and *B* : Organic matter

20. What happens when a solution of an acid (hydrochloric acid) is mixed with a solution of a base (sodium hydroxide). The equation given below is

Sodium hydroxide + Hydrochloric acid $\longrightarrow$ Sodium chloride + Water

I. The temperature of the solution increases.

II. The temperature of the solution decreases.

III. The temperature of the solution remains the same.

IV. Salt formation takes place.

Codes

(a) Only I   (b) I and III
(c) II and III   (d) I and IV

21. Rama found that an ant bites on her hand. She immediately rubbed some baking powder over it and get relief from pain and irritation. She do so to neutralise the acid injected by ant by the base. The compound formed after neutralisation has the formula

(a) NaCl   (b) CH_3COONa
(c) HCOONa   (d) Cannot be predicted

2 Marks Questions

22. Match the salts given in Column I with their formula given in Column II and choose the correct answer using the codes given below:

	Column I		**Column II**
A.	Limestone	1.	$CuSO_4 \cdot 5H_2O$
B.	Blue vitriol	2.	$CaSO_4 \cdot 2H_2O$
C.	Washing soda	3.	$CaCO_3$
D.	Baking soda	4.	$NaHCO_3$
		5.	$Na_2CO_3 \cdot 10H_2O$

Codes

	A	B	C	D			A	B	C	D
(a)	2	1	5	4		(b)	3	1	4	5
(c)	1	2	5	4		(d)	3	1	5	4

23. Match the acids given in Column I with their applications given in Column II and choose the correct answer using the codes given below.

	Column I (Acids)		**Column II** (Uses)
A.	Hydrochloric acid	1.	In storage batteries
B.	Sulphuric acid	2.	Present in yoghurt
C.	Lactic acid	3.	In making vinegar
D.	Acetic acid	4.	As bathroom acid

Codes

	A	B	C	D			A	B	C	D
(a)	4	1	2	3		(b)	4	1	3	2
(c)	1	4	2	3		(d)	4	2	1	3

24.

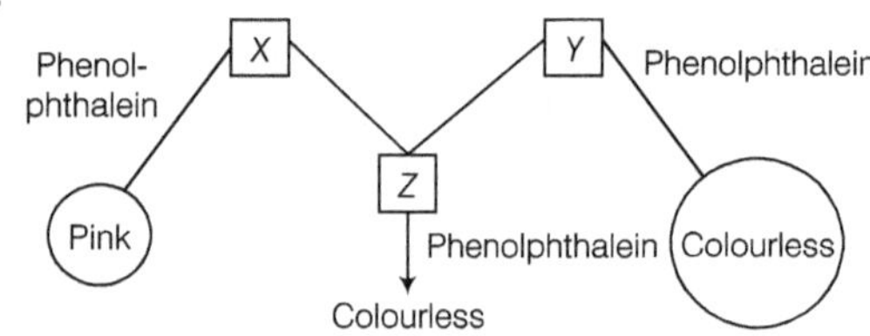

X, Y and Z are

	X	Y	Z
(a)	CuO	H_2SO_4	$CuSO_4$
(b)	NaCl	HCl	NaOH
(c)	H_2SO_4	CuO	$CuSO_4$
(d)	HCl	NaOH	NaCl

25. Complete the following paragraph by selecting appropriate words for P, Q, R and S. P alongwith Q are obtained when hydrochloric acid reacts with sodium hydroxide. The process is R and resulting in a S solution.

	P	Q	R	S
(a)	Salt	water	exothermic	neutral
(b)	Salt	water	endothermic	acidic
(c)	Salt	water	endothermic	neutral
(d)	Salt	water	exothermic	acidic

Physical and Chemical Changes

1 Mark Questions

1. Consider the following properties.
   I. Colour   II. Shape   III. Size
   Which of these are affected during a physical change?
   (a) I and II
   (b) II and III
   (c) I and III
   (d) I, II and III

2. Melting, boiling, freezing and P are all examples of Q. Here, P and Q, respectively are
   (a) electrolysis, oxidation
   (b) photosynthesis, natural changes
   (c) expansion, physical changes
   (d) precipitation, chemical changes

3. Which of the following are the examples of physical change?
   I. Switching on a light bulb.
   II. Making yoghurt at home.
   III. The ripening of some bananas that were left on the kitchen counter top.
   IV. Ironing a wrinkled T-shirt.
   Codes
   (a) I and IV   (b) II and III
   (c) I, III and IV   (d) None of these

4. Paheli's mother made a concentrated sugar syrup by dissolving sugar in hot water. On cooling, crystals of sugar got separated. This indicates a
   (a) physical change that can be reversed
   (b) chemical change that can be reversed
   (c) physical change that cannot be reversed
   (d) chemical change that cannot be reversed

5. Choose among the following, one that shows a correct match between chemical/physical change and energy transformation.
   (a) Sandling wood : physical change, energy absorbed
   (b) Burning coal : chemical change, exothermic
   (c) Melting ice : physical change, energy released
   (d) Digestion of food : chemical change, endothermic

6. Richa adds some common salt in water and stirs the solution. During this process,
   I. a new substance is obtained.
   II. the change is temporary.
   III. salt retains its chemical properties.

IV. the change is permanent.

The true observations are

(a) I and II   (b) I and IV
(c) II and III   (d) II and IV

7. Sohan filled an ice tray with water and kept it in the freezer for about 2 hours. The change observed by him (according to his view) are

I. a solid is obtained.

II. the movement of particles in the product decreases.

III. the force of attraction between the water molecules decreases.

IV. a new substance is formed.

The correct observations are

(a) I and II   (b) I, II and III
(c) I and IV   (d) I, II and IV

8. The following are generally observed during a process.

I. Heat   II. Sound   III. Gas

Which of the above can accompany a chemical change?

(a) I and II   (b) II and III
(c) I and III   (d) All of these

9. Seema took some pickle from the burney by using metal spoon, but she left the spoon there. After a few days, when she again took the pickle, she found the spoon but with a hole. What could be the possible reason for this?

(a) Metal is dissolved by the oil present in the pickle

(b) Metal is dissolved by a gas which is liberated by the oil in the presence of metal

(c) Metal reacts with the acid present in the pickle to form salt and hence, gets dissolved

(d) Metal reacts with the burney material (glass) to give acid which dissolves the metal

10. Shruti took a mixture of sulphur powder and iron turning. She could separate them with the help of magnet. Then, she heated the mixture. After heating, she tried to separate the iron turning by using magnet but she failed. This is because

(a) heating results in the formation of a new substance

(b) heating changes the nature of iron, so it is not attracted by magnet

(c) heating results in evaporation of iron and sulphur is left behind

(d) heating melts the sulphur in which iron gets dissolved

11. Consider the following processes.

I. Obtaining salt from sea water.

II. Snow flakes formation.

III. Obtaining sugar from sugar syrup.

IV. Formation of rust over iron surface.

The crystallisation processes among the above are

(a) I and II

(b) II and III

(c) I, II and III

(d) All of the above

12. Which of the following statements about chemical changes is/are not correct?

I. Mixing oil and water is an example of a chemical change.

II. A chemical change is also known as a permanent change.

III. New substances may or may not be formed.

IV. Heat energy is always given out to the surroundings.

Codes

(a) Only I   (b) II and III
(c) I, III and IV   (d) All of the given

13. Consider the following processes.

   I. Dissolution of sugar in water

   II. Formation of clouds

   III. Cooking of food

   IV. Respiration

   V. Photosynthesis

The processes occurring with change in composition is/are

(a) I, II and III   (b) III, IV and V
(c) II, IV and V   (d) None of these

14. Consider the following statements.

   I. Crystallisation is a permanent change.

   II. Digestion involves formation of a new substance.

   III. Burning of paper is a chemical change.

   IV. A chemical change is always reversible.

The correct statement (s) among the above is/are

(a) I and III   (b) II, III and IV
(c) II and III   (d) Only IV

15. Which of the following is/are the example(s) of chemical changes?

   I. Melting of candle wax when heated.

   II. Iodine crystals forming a purple vapour upon heating.

   III. Dissolving magnesium ribbon in hydrochloric acid.

   IV. Copper carbonate turns into a black powder upon heating.

Codes

(a) I and II   (b) III and IV
(c) II, III and IV   (d) All of the given

16. A man painted his main gate made up of iron, to

   I. prevent it from rusting.

   II. protect it from sun.

   III. make it look beautiful.

   IV. make it dust free.

Which of the above statement(s) is/are correct?

(a) I and II   (b) II and III
(c) Only II   (d) I and III

17. The gas we use in the kitchen is called Liquefied Petroleum Gas (LPG). In the cylinder, it exists as liquid. When it comes out from the cylinder, it becomes a gas (Change – A) then it burns (Change – B). The following statements pertain to these changes. Choose the correct one.

(a) Processes A are a chemical change
(b) Processes B are a physical change
(c) Processes A is a physical change but B is a chemical change
(d) Process A is a chemical change but B is a physical change

18. Seema took a wooden log and try the following experiments.

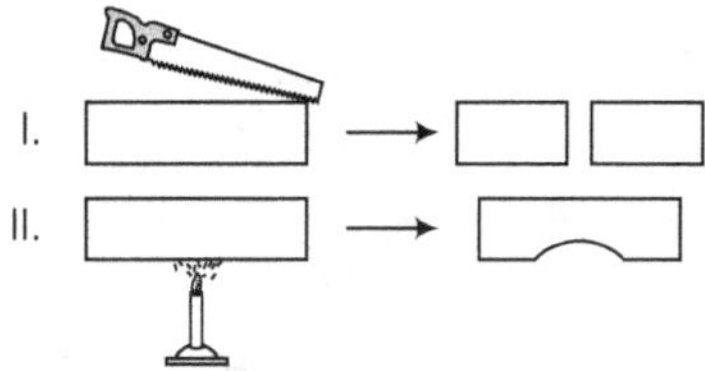

Are the above two experiments involve same type of changes and why?
(a) Yes, as both are physical changes
(b) No, as I is physical but II is chemical change
(c) Yes, as both are chemical changes
(d) No, as I is chemical but II is physical change

19. In a pressure kerosene stove, following processes take place.

   I. The stove is pumped to convert kerosene into vapours.

   II. The vapours are then ignited.

The true statement about the above two changes is

(a) I is a chemical change and II is a physical change

(b) I is a physical change and II is a chemical change

(c) I and II both are physical changes

(d) I and II both are chemical changes

20. Match the items of Column I with the items of Column II and choose the correct answer using the codes given below.

	Column I		Column II
A.	Depositing a layer of zinc on iron	1.	Rust
B.	Iron oxide	2.	Chemical change
C.	Dissolving common salt in water	3.	Galvanisation
D.	Souring of milk	4.	Physical change

Codes

	A	B	C	D		A	B	C	D
(a)	3	2	4	1	(b)	4	1	2	3
(c)	3	1	4	2	(d)	4	2	3	1

2 Marks Questions

21. Refer to the given Venn diagram and identify X.

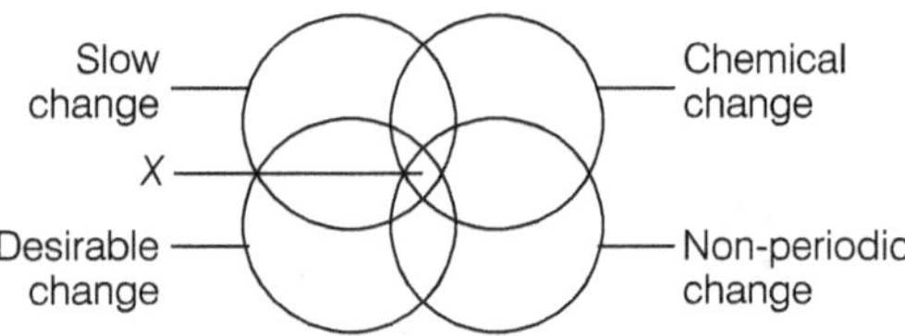

(a) Eruption of volcanoes

(b) Burning of paper

(c) Rusting of bicycle

(d) Ripening of guava

22. Which portion of a ship shown below will rust the fastest?

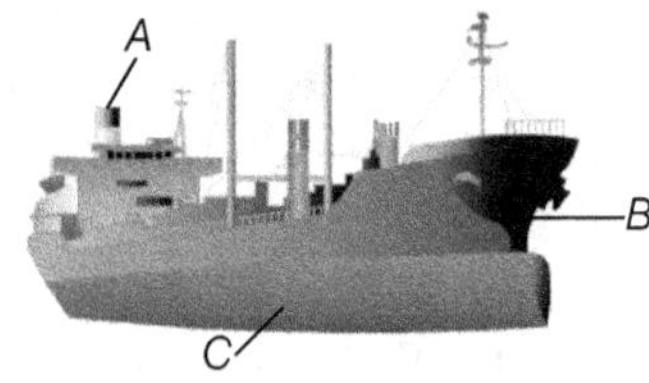

(a) A

(b) B

(c) C

(d) A, B, C will get rust equilly

23. Observe the given figure carefully

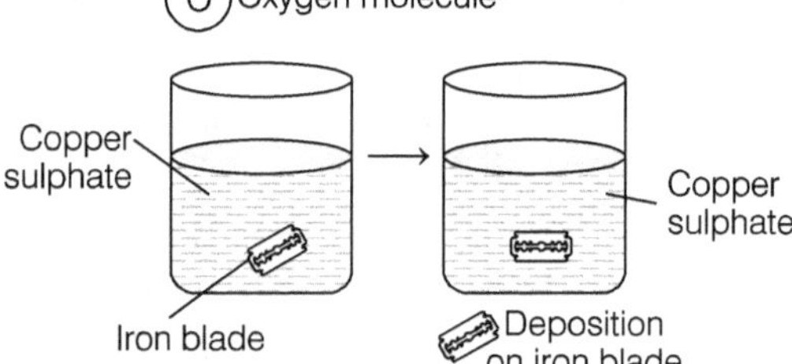

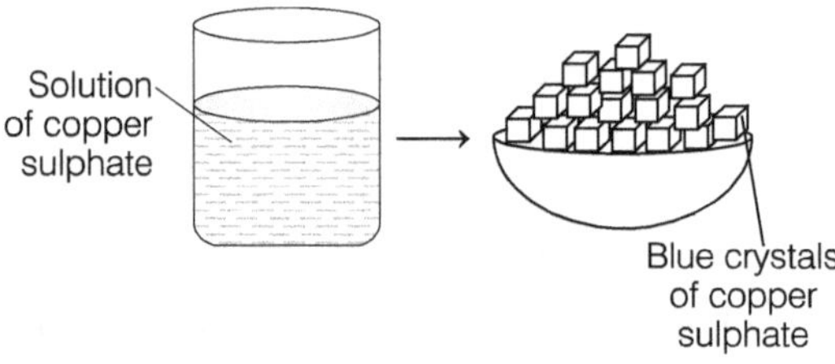

Which of the following statements is incorrect regarding the process shown in figure A and B?

(a) A new substance is formed in both the process.

(b) Iron blade undergoes rusting and a brown deposition is formed on it.

(c) Process in figure *A* is irreversible while that in figure *B* is reversible.

(d) All of the above

24. Match the processes given in Column I with their type given in Column II and choose the correct answer using the codes given below.

	Column I		Column II
A.	Heating a metal for expansion	1.	Physical change
B.	Placing a stone in sunlight	2.	Chemical change
C.	Burning of kerosene in stove	3.	Both physical and chemical change
D.	Curdling of milk	4.	Neither physical nor chemical change

Codes

	A	B	C	D
(a)	1	3	4	2
(b)	1	2	4	3
(c)	1	4	3	2
(d)	1	3	2	4

25. What causes the candle flame to get extinguished?

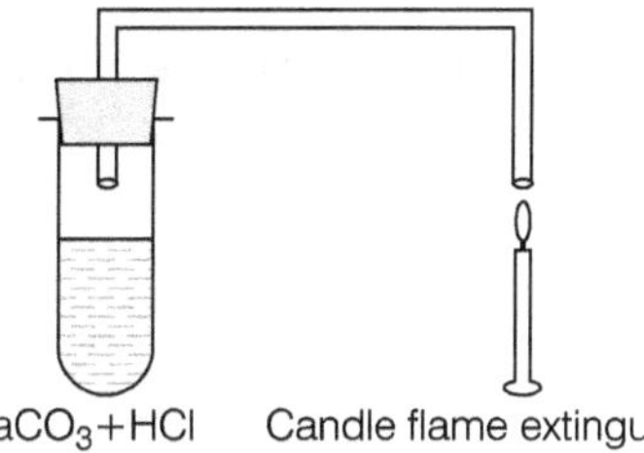

(a) Evolution of O_2 gas

(b) Evolution of CO_2 gas

(c) Formation of $Ca(OH)_2$

(d) Formation of $CaCl_2$

Weather, Climate and Adaptations of Animals to Climate

1 Mark Questions

1. Hot and dry climate can be associated with which of the following regions?
   (a) Desert
   (b) Tropic
   (c) Arctic
   (d) Temperate region

2. The temperature of a region is high most of the time, and it receives heavy rainfall on most of the days. The climate of this region is
   (a) hot and wet
   (b) hot and dry
   (c) very hot in summer and very cold in winters
   (d) extremely cold and dry

3. As we move away from the equator, the temperature will
   (a) increase
   (b) decrease
   (c) cannot be predicted
   (d) show no changes

4. Pawan while visiting a national park observed a wide variety of dense flora and fauna flourishing together.
   On the basis of his observation, identify the most likely location of this national park and select the correct option.
   (a) Arctic
   (b) Tropic
   (c) Desert
   (d) Coastal area

5. The animals living in polar regions are known to have a thick layer of fat under their furs. This layer helps by
   (a) increasing the heat loss
   (b) exchanging their swimming skills
   (c) insulating the body
   (d) protecting from predators

6. An animal adapted to arboreal habitat in tropics should be
   (a) expert climber
   (b) frugivorous
   (c) sharp sighted
   (d) All of these

7. Which of the following characterstics is true for an animal that has gone under hibernation?
   (a) Long period of inactivity
   (b) Increased metabolism
   (c) Intermittent periods of activity
   (d) Movement to warmer places

8. A carnivore animal with strips all over its body, that can move extremely fast to catch a prey is most likely found in
   (a) Sahara desert
   (b) North pole
   (c) Western Ghats
   (d) Oceans

9. Lions and elephants are animals living in rainforests on land. However there is no competition observed between these two animals. The most possible explanation for this is
(a) different food habits
(b) ability to camouflage
(c) different habitats
(d) Seasonal migration of elephants

10.

Which of the following statements correctly indicates a similarity between the two animals shown above?
(a) They move very slowly
(b) Eyes are in front of head
(c) They have a unique foot structure
(d) They remain inactive during the day

11. Some of the adaptations in animals are given below.

White fur, frugivorous, sticky pads on feet, thick skin, strong tails, strong sense of smell, long and large beak

How many of these adaptations are for habitats present in tropical rainforests?
(a) 5   (b) 7   (c) 4   (d) 3

12. Match the following columns.

	Column I		Column II
A.	Wind speed	1.	Hygrometer
B.	Air pressure	2.	Thermometer
C.	Precipitation	3.	Barometer
D.	Temperature	4.	Anemometer
		5.	Rain gauze

Codes

	A	B	C	D			A	B	C	D
(a)	4	3	5	2		(b)	1	2	3	4
(c)	2	5	4	1		(d)	3	1	2	5

2 Marks Questions

13. Read the given statements and select the option which correctly identifies each statement as True (T) or False (F).
  I. Weather is constant everywhere.
  II. Humidity is the measure of amount of air in the atmosphere.
  III. Weather is an average climatic conditions of an area over a period of time.
  IV. Hill stations always have a cool climate.

Codes

	I	II	III	IV			I	II	III	IV
(a)	T	T	T	F		(b)	F	F	F	T
(c)	T	F	T	F		(d)	F	T	F	T

14. Two types of animals P and Q live in tropical rainforests. P is a very large and heavy animal, preventing it from sinking in soft ground, while Q is a colourful bird with strange beak, it can get food from trees that not easily reachable.

Select the option which correctly identifies P and Q.

	P	Q
(a)	Lion	Lion tailed macaque
(b)	Elephant	Toucan
(c)	Red eyes frog	Penguin
(d)	Polar bears	Monkey

15. Read the following statements.

I. Reduced metabolic activity during process X helps animal Y to escape harsh winters.

II. Process X is of a longer duration, i.e. lasts for an entire season.

Choose the correct statement regarding X and Y.

(a) X could be aestivation exhibited by animal Y, i.e. tortoise.

(b) X could be migration exhibited by animal Y, i.e. penguins to escape winters.

(c) X could be hibernation exhibited by animal Y, i.e. polar bears.

(d) X could be aestivation exhibited by animal Y, i.e. a snake.

16. One of the most common migratory bird is the Siberian crane which comes to India, every year for a few months. How do these birds travel to same place year after year?

I. They have an inbuilt sense of direction.

II. They are guided by the position of Sun.

III. Its a trial and error process.

Codes

(a) Only I

(b) Only II

(c) All three

(d) I and II

17. Ravi categorised different animals on the basis of the habitats they live in. He added three names to each of the three groups he created. However, one wrong name got added to each of these pairs. Identify it and select the correct option.

Group I - Macaw, Lion tailed macaque, Kangaroo rat

Group II - Monkeys, Polar bears, Toucan

Group III - Camel, Seal, Elephant

(a) Kangaroo rat of group I should be changed with seal of group II.

(b) Seal of group III should be changed with toucan of group II.

(c) Kangaroo rat of group I should be changed with elephant of group III.

(d) Polar bears of group II should be changed with seal in group III.

Wind, Storms and Cyclone

1 Mark Questions

1. Which of the following is responsible for all the changes in weather?
   (a) Rain   (b) Sun   (c) Wind (d) Vapour

2. Tornadoes are dark funnel-shaped clouds that reach from
   (a) the sky to the ground
   (b) the ground to the sky
   (c) the sky to the sea
   (d) the sea to the sky

3. How many wind belts are there on Earth?
   (a) Four   (b) Two   (c) One   (d) Three

4. While going to school or elsewhere you must have seen that holes are made in hanging banners and hoarding, which of the following can be the reason behind it?
   (a) To bind it tightly
   (b) So, that high speed wind can pass through it
   (c) To beautify them
   (d) None of the above

5. "Warm air is lighter than cold air" which of the following can satisfy the above statement?
   (a) Process of evaporation
   (b) Process of condensation
   (c) Rise of smoke in air
   (d) Both (a) and (c)

6. What is/are the factors contribute in development of cyclone?
   (a) Wind speed
   (b) Wind direction
   (c) Temperature and humidity
   (d) All of the above

7. Which of the following defines the lightning correctly?
   (a) Accumulation of electric charge
   (b) Light waves
   (c) Discharge of electric charges
   (d) Flow of charge

8. At what condition the thunderstorm becomes cyclone?
   (a) Low pressure system and low wind speed.
   (b) High pressure system and low wind speed.
   (c) Low pressure system and high wind speed.
   (d) High pressure system and low wind speed.

9. Rohan is a naughty boy, one day he takes a can of water and heat it in microwave. After heating it, he put the can under the running water. He observe the shape of tin can is distorted?

   The next day he ask his teacher how the shape of tin can distorted.

What reason did his teacher give him?
(a) Due to the excess pressure outside the can.
(b) Due to the reduced pressure outside the can.
(c) Due to equal pressure
(d) None of the above

10. Which of the following term is given for the forces generated due to Earth's revolution?
(a) Greenhouse effect
(b) Coriolis effect
(c) EL Nino effect
(d) La Nino effect

11. The winds moving from West to East between 30° and 60° latitude are known as
(a) Trade winds
(b) Polar wind
(c) Westerly winds
(d) Local wind

12. Choose the correct statement regarding the figures given below.
I. The given figure *A* is called aminometer.
II. *A* is used to measure the speed of wind.
III. The wind wave used to determine the direction of wind.

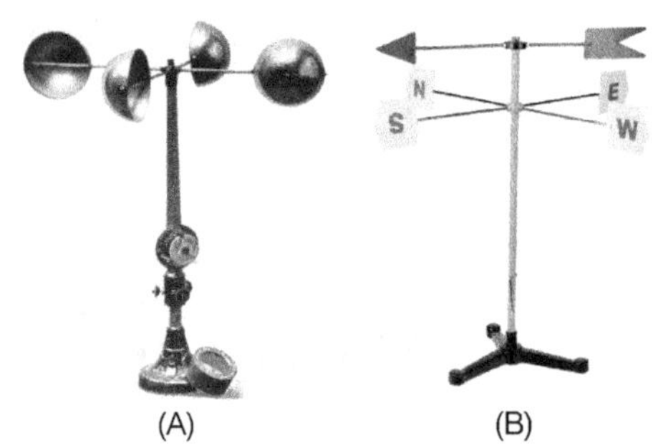

Codes
(a) I and II
(b) II and III
(c) Only III
(d) Only I

13. Which is correct about thunderstorm?
I. It is accompanied by thunder and lightning.
II. It develops in hot and humid area.
III. A cyclone becomes thunderstorm when a high pressure is accompanied by low speed winds.
Codes
(a) I and II
(b) II and III
(c) I and III
(d) I, II and III

2 Marks Questions

14. State whether the following are True (T) or False (F).
I. With increase in temperature the air expands.
II. Increase wind speed is accompanied by increase pressure.
III. Greater the difference in pressure, the faster the air moves.
IV. Monsoon blows from sea towards the land in winter.

Codes

	I	II	III	IV
(a)	T	F	T	F
(b)	T	T	F	T
(c)	F	T	T	F
(d)	T	T	F	F

15. Aman took three test tubes X, Y and Z filled with hot water, normal water and chilled water respectively. He fixed balloons on the mouth of each test tube.

Now, identify the correct statement regarding X, Y and Z.
(a) X-will remain same, Y-will inflate
(b) Y-will deflate, Z-will inflate
(c) X-will inflate, Z-will remain same
(d) None of these will inflate

16. Match the Column I with Column II.

	Column I		Column II
A.	Typhoon	1.	Instrument used to measure wind speed.
B.	Anemometer	2.	Monsoon
C.	Difference in air pressure in nature	3.	Alternative name of cyclone.
D.	Wind carrying water	4.	Created due to difference in temperature.
E.	High speed wind	5.	Accompained by low pressure.

Codes

	A	B	C	D	E
(a)	3	2	1	4	5
(b)	5	4	3	1	2
(c)	5	1	3	2	4
(d)	3	1	4	2	5

17. Anshu take two paper bags and hang them in inverted position on the two ends of a metal. She put burning candle below one of the bag as shown in figure.

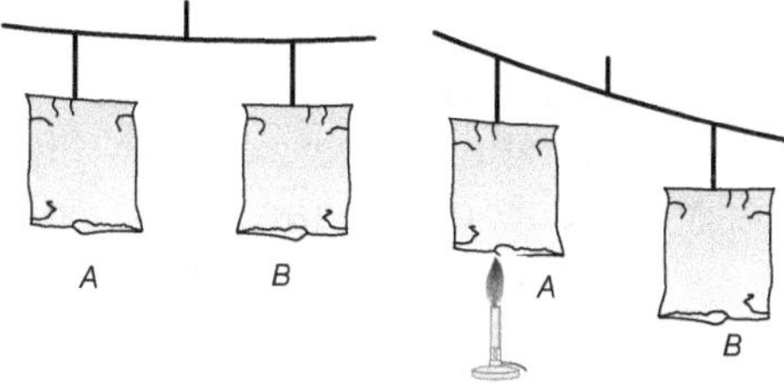

after some time the bag A lifted above. Which property of air this experiment shows?
(a) Air expands and rises up on heating
(b) Air contact and falls down on heating
(c) Both (a) and (b)
(d) None of the above

Respiration in Human Beings and Animals

1 Mark Questions

1. Observe the figure given below and mark the correct option that shows the part of human respiratory system involved in exchange of gases.

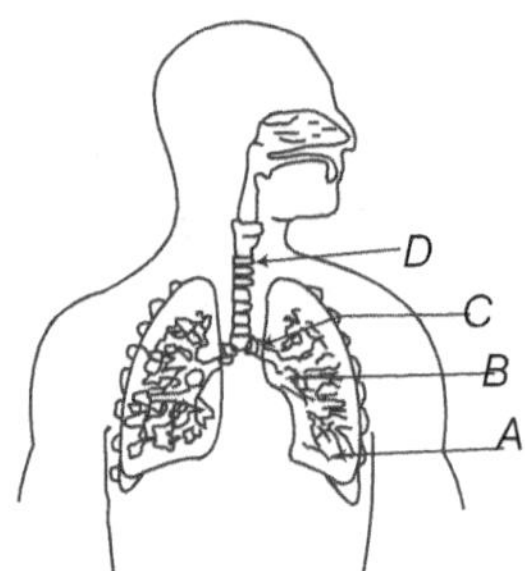

Codes
(a) A (b) C
(c) B (d) D

2. Given below are the parts of human respiratory system.

  (i) Nostrils   (ii) Trachea
(iii) Pharynx   (iv) Bronchi
  (v) Lungs

In what order will the oxygen inhaled passes through these structures?
(a) i → ii → iii → iv → v
(b) i → iii → ii → iv → v
(c) i → iv → ii → iii → v
(d) i → iii → iv → ii → v

3. After heavy exercise, people often complain of cramps in leg muscles. The most plausible reason for this is
(a) accumulation of alcohol in muscles.
(b) low level of CO_2 in muscles.
(c) accumulation of lactic acid in muscles.
(d) high level of CO_2 in muscles.

4. In yeast, the process of respiration takes place in the absence of oxygen unlike in humans. Which of the following correctly indicates this type of respiration?
(a) Glucose $\longrightarrow CO_2$ + Water + Energy
(b) Glucose $\longrightarrow$ Lactic acid + Energy
(c) Glucose $\longrightarrow$ Ethyl alcohol + CO_2 + Energy
(d) Glucose $\xrightarrow{CO_2}$ Lactic acid + Energy

5. In an animal, for respiration, oxygen rich air rushes through P into the Q, diffuses into R and reaches every cell of the body.
(a) $P →$ Spiracles, $Q →$ Tracheal tubes, $R →$ Body tissue
(b) $P →$ Tracheal tubes, $P →$ Spiracles, $R →$ Body cells
(c) $P →$ Body tissue, $Q →$ Trachea, $P →$ Spiracles
(d) None of the above

6. Given below are two events that take place during respiration
   I. Ribs are pushed upward and outward.
   II. Air pressure decreases inside the lungs.
   These two envents take place during
   (a) heavy physical exercise
   (b) inhalation
   (c) exhalation
   (d) Both (b) and (c)

7. A person's nose was clipped and was asked to breathe in and out in a plastic bag.
   Which of the following changes in the blood of the person could be the reason for the change in his breathing rate and deep breathing?
   (a) The carbon dioxide concentration had increased.
   (b) The lactic acid concentration had increased.
   (c) The oxygen concentration had increased.
   (d) The temperature of his blood had increased.

8. Which of the following is not a cause for the increase in blood flow to the skeletal muscle during exercise?
   (a) Increase in heart rate
   (b) Increase in blood pressure
   (c) Increase in breathing rate
   (d) Dilation of arteries in the muscle

9. Which of the following reasons are for increase in blood flow through the skeletal muscle during exercise?
   I. To remove more urea from the muscle.
   II. To carry more heat away from the muscle.
   III. To increase the oxygen supply to the muscle.

Codes
   (a) I and II   (b) II and III
   (c) I and III   (d) I, II and III

10. Read the following statements w.r.t structure X.
   I. X are present on leaf surface and young stems.
   II. It helps in gaseous exchange within plants.
   III. X are surrounded by guard cells which control its movement.
   Structure X is correctly identified as
   (a) Stomata   (b) Lenticels
   (c) Roots   (d) Root hairs

11. If a potted plant is overwatered for a long time, it may ultimately die. The most plausible reason for this observation is
   I. Water expels the air between soil particles.
   II. Sufficient O_2 supply.
   III. Anaerobic respiration by plant roots.
   Codes
   (a) Only I   (b) II and III
   (c) I and II   (d) I and III

12. Refer to the figure given below. Select the statement which is incorrect w.r.t figure A and B.

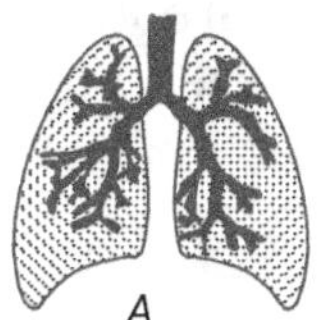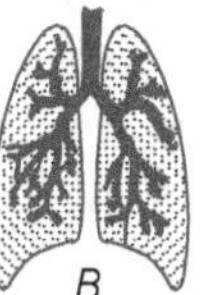

   (a) Diaphragm becomes flat in A, while dome-shaped in B.
   (b) Muscles between ribs contract in A but relax in B.
   (c) Volume of thoracic cavity decrease in A and increases in B.
   (d) Ribcage moves up and out in A but down and inwards in B.

13. The diagram below shows a section through the human thorax. Two sets of muscles are labelled as *P* and *Q* and the thoracic cavity is labelled as *R*.

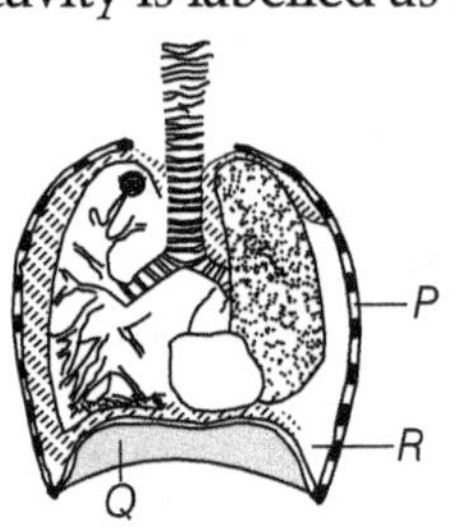

Which of the following occurs in them for air to enter the lungs?

	Muscles *P*	Muscles *Q*	Volume of *R*
(a)	Relax	Contract	Increased
(b)	Contract	Contract	Increased
(c)	Contract	Relax	Reduced
(d)	Relax	Relax	Increase

2 Marks Questions

14. Match the columns and select the correct option.

	Column I		Column II
A.	Birds	1.	Gills
B.	Cockroach	2.	Lungs
C.	Earthworm	3.	Tracheal
D.	Dolphin	4.	Blow holes
E.	Fish	5.	Skin

Codes

	A	B	C	D	E
(a)	4	2	3	5	1
(b)	1	3	2	4	4
(c)	2	3	5	4	1
(d)	3	1	4	2	5

15. The flow chart shows how the element carbon, present in carbon dioxide and carbohydrates is passed on to the environment

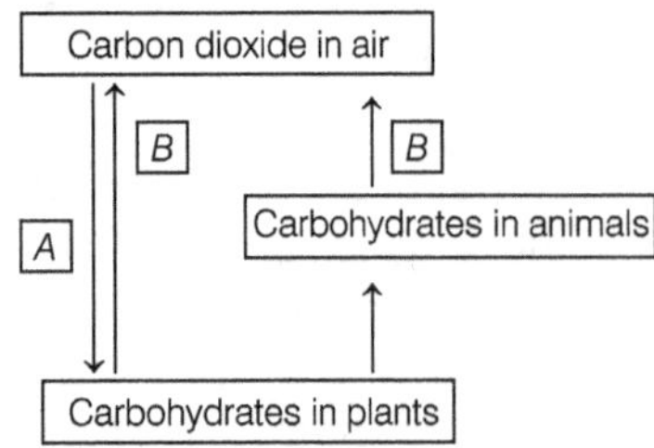

Identify processes *A* and *B*.

	A	*B*
(a)	Respiration	Photosynthesis
(b)	Photosynthesis	Respiration
(c)	Aerobic respiration	Photosynthesis
(d)	Transpiration	Aerobic respiration

16. Observe the flow chart given below and identify *P*, *Q*, *R* and *S* by analysing the options that follows.

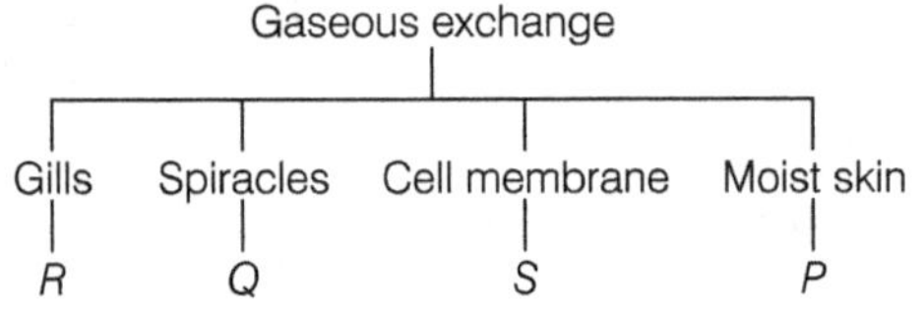

Codes

	P	*Q*	*R*	*S*
(a)	Pigeon	Cockroach	Tadpole	Earthworm
(b)	Frog	Grasshopper	Fish	*Amoeba*
(c)	Crab	Spider	Frog	*Paramecium*
(d)	Penguin	Mynah	Snake	Leech

Transportation in Animals and Plants

1 Mark Questions

1. I am a part of the circulatory system, present in the chest cavity and work continuously for normal functioning of the body. Who am I?
   (a) Kidney (b) Heart
   (c) Lungs (d) Blood

2. In human body, which part helps in eliminating wastes?
   A. Kidney B. Heart
   C. Skin D. Stomach
   Codes
   (a) A and B (b) A and C
   (c) B and D (d) C and D

3. If a person is unable to produce white blood cells in their body, which of the following is the most likely consequence in this situation?
   (a) Low level of blood oxygen
   (b) Inability of the blood to clot
   (c) Decrease level of immunity
   (d) Change in colour of blood

4. Part *A* forms a continuous network of channels connecting roots to the leaves through stems and branches to transport water and minerals to entire plant. Part *A* can be identified as
   (a) Stomata
   (b) Phloem
   (c) Roots
   (d) Xylem

5. Refer the given experimental set up prepared by a group of students and select the correct option for the following question.

   Why do we notice tiny droplets of water on the inner surface of the glass cover?
   (a) Due to photolysis
   (b) Due to transpiration
   (c) Due to photorespiration
   (d) Due to photosynthesis

6. In order to increase the rate of water absorption through the roots, a potted plant can be kept
   (a) in shade
   (b) in dimly lit area
   (c) under a fan
   (d) covered with a plastic bag

7. Read the characteristics of a plant part given below.

   I. Increase the surface area of water absorption.

  II. In direct contact with soil particles.

This part is

(a) leaves

(b) roots

(c) stems

(d) root hairs

8. Which of the following transports are conducted by the plasma component of blood?

	Oxygen	CO_2	Heat	Nitrogenous waste
(a)	✓	✓	✗	✓
(b)	✗	✓	✓	✓
(c)	✗	✓	✗	✓
(d)	✓	✓	✓	✓

9. In the figure below, which of the labelled portion carries deoxygenated blood to lungs?

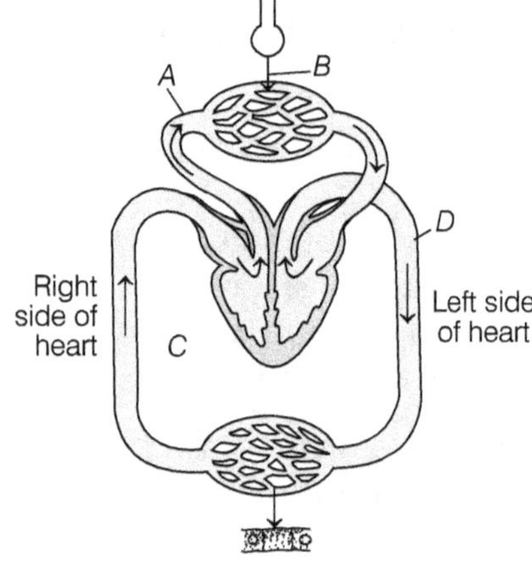

(a) *A* and *B*

(b) *B* and *C*

(c) *C* and *A*

(d) *D* and *B*

10. Refer to the figure given below.

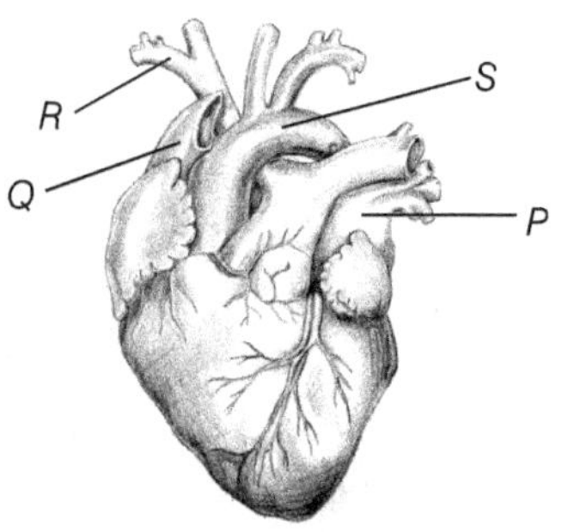

Which of the following labels correctly identifies with blood vessel carrying impure blood from heart to lungs?

(a) *Q*-Vena cava

(b) *R*-Pulmonary artery

(c) *S*-Aorta

(d) *P*-Pulmonary vein

11. The diagram shows blood as seen under a microscope.

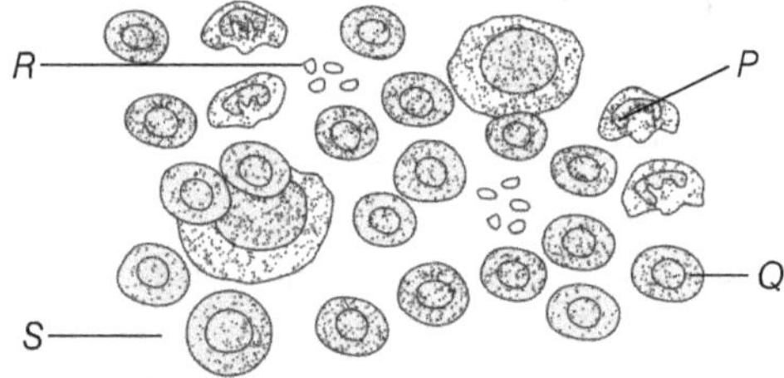

Identify the option which is correct w.r.t *P, Q, R* and *S*.

(a) *P*-Blood which carries different types of cells.

(b) *R*-Platelets whose count reduces in case of infections.

(c) *S*-WBCs whose lowered count results in excessive blood loss.

(d) *Q*-RBC which supplies oxygen to all cells of the body.

12. Given below are parts involved in flow of blood throughout the human circulatory system.

   I. Left atrium   II. Right ventricle

III. Lungs

IV. Left ventricle

V. Right atrium

Select the correct option which identifies the order in which the blood flows through these parts?

(a) I $\rightarrow$ IV $\rightarrow$ III $\rightarrow$ V $\rightarrow$ II

(b) IV $\rightarrow$ I $\rightarrow$ III $\rightarrow$ II $\rightarrow$ V

(c) V $\rightarrow$ II $\rightarrow$ III $\rightarrow$ I $\rightarrow$ IV

(d) II $\rightarrow$ V $\rightarrow$ III $\rightarrow$ II $\rightarrow$ I

13. Select the correct combination.

I. Urethra: Duct leading from the urinary bladder to outside the body.

II. Ureter: Tube that carries urine from urethra to urinary bladder.

III. Urinary bladder: Hollow muscular sac located in pelvis.

IV. Nephron: Filtering unit of kidney.

Codes

(a) I and II

(b) I, III and IV

(c) III and IV

(d) All are correct

14. Which of the following combination are correct?

	Part of plants	Functions
A	Stomata	Transpiration
B	Xylem	Transport of oxygen
C	Phloem	Transport of food
D	Root hair	Gaseous exchange

Codes

(a) A and B (b) B and C

(c) A and C (d) A, B and D

15. Which of the following statement(s) is/are incorrect?

I. Plants produce excretory product like resins, gums, etc.

II. Water evaporates through the stomata by the process of transpiration.

III. Gaseous exchange in plants take place through stomata.

IV. Transpiration is a process in plants that allow it to grow.

V. CO_2 is released through the stomata during photosynthesis.

VI. A suction pull helps to pass the food through phloem.

Codes

(a) I, II and III

(b) IV, V and VI

(c) I, III and V

(d) II, IV and VI

16. Three set ups X, Y and Z are prepared as shown below.

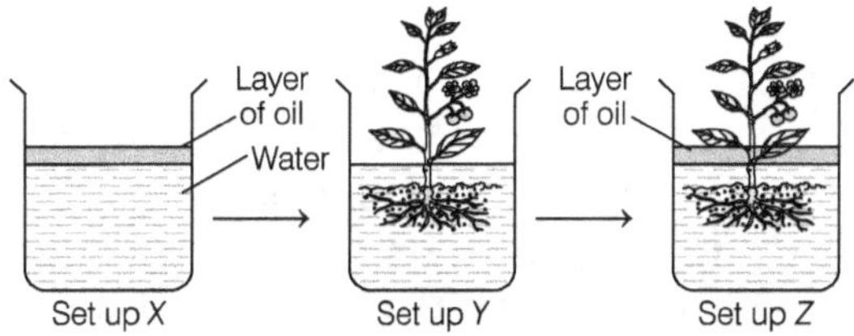

Select the option which identifies the rate of water loss from all the set ups in decreasing order.

(a) X, Y and Z

(b) Y, Z and X

(c) X, Z and Y

(d) Z, Y and X

2 Marks Questions

17. Observe the diagram given below and select the option that correctly declares the waste product at the end of the flow chart.

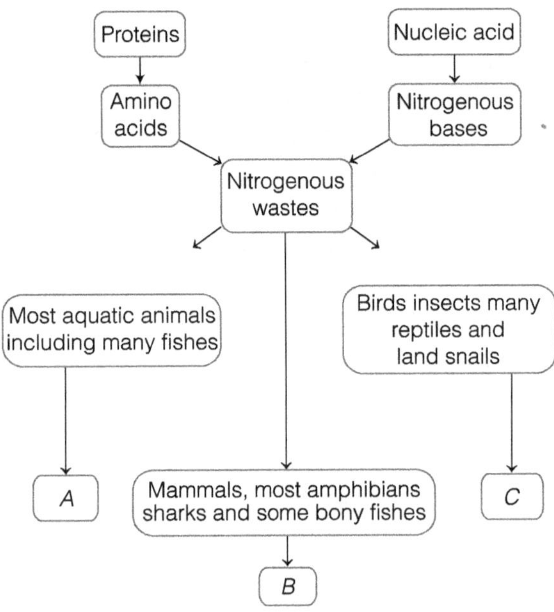

Codes

	A	B	C
(a)	Ammonia	Urea	Uric acid
(b)	Urea	Ammonia	Uric acid
(c)	Uric acid	Urea	Ammonia
(d)	Ammonia	Uric acid	Urea

18. The figure given below shows a type of blood vessels, labelled as X. Which of the following from the codes is an incorrect statement w.r.t to the vessel X.

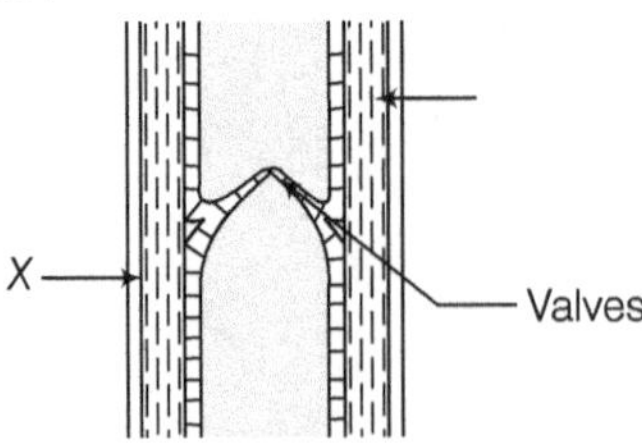

I. It carry blood to the heart.

II. It have thick walls.

III. It is superficially placed.

IV. It is identified as veins.

Codes

   (a) I and II   (b) Only III
   (c) III and IV   (d) Only II

19. Refer to the figure given below and select the correct statement.

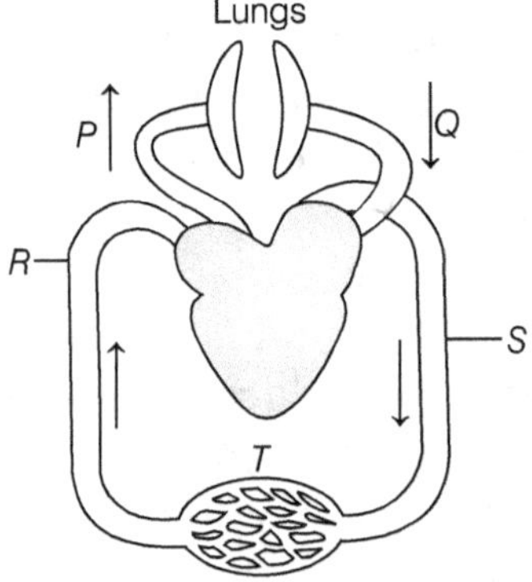

(a) R does not have valves, while S has them to prevent back flow of blood.

(b) In the absence of T, body cells can receive nutrients but elimination of waste well remain unaffected.

(c) CO_2 rich blood from body and O_2 rich blood from lungs mixes in the heart.

(d) In our body, blood enters twice in the heart for one complete circulation.

20. Read the statements given below with respect to movement X and Y.

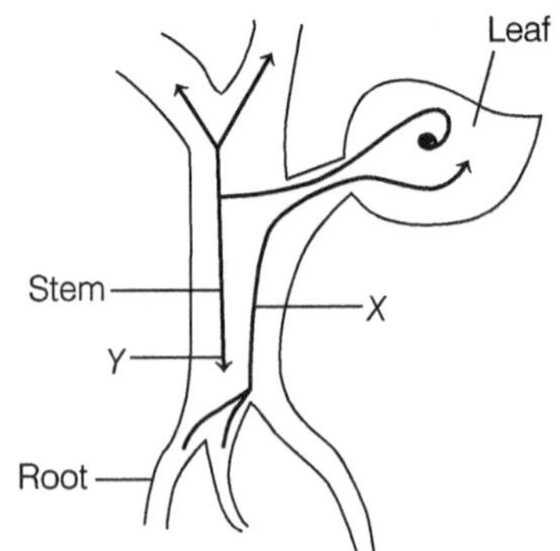

I. In movement Y, food prepared by leaves gets transported to all parts through xylem.

II. In movement X, water and dissolved minerals are transported from root to leaves of a plant

Select the correct option.

(a) I is correct, II is incorrect
(b) I is incorrect, II is correct
(c) Both statements are correct
(d) Both statements are incorrect

21. Observe the given figure, which shows different parts of the heart. Select the option that correctly matches the labels P, Q, R and S in the figure with the given list (A – D).

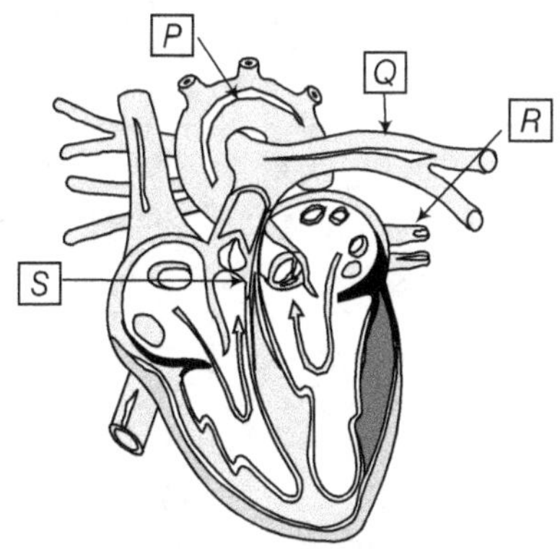

A. It carries blood to different parts of the body.

B. It brings back oxygen rich blood from the lungs.

C. They allow the blood to flow only in one direction.

D. It avoid mixing of deoxygenated and oxygenated blood in our heart.

Codes
(a) $P - B$, $Q - D$, $R - A$, $S - C$
(b) $P - A$, $Q - B$, $R - C$, $S - D$
(c) $P - D$, $Q - A$, $R - B$, $S - C$
(d) $P - A$, $Q - D$, $R - B$, $S - C$

22. A plant is left under the hot Sun for 6 hours. The figure given below shows the change in appearance of the plant during this period.

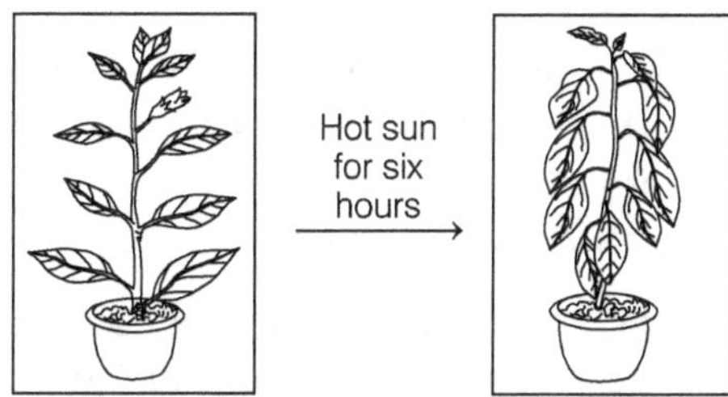

Which of the following statements correctly explain the change in appearance of this plant?

I. More water is lost by transpiration than water that is absorbed.

II. Stomata are closed at this time.

III. Conduction of water and organic solutes through xylem has stopped.

Codes
(a) I and II   (b) Only I
(c) Only II   (d) I, II and III

Reproduction in Plants

1 Mark Questions

1. Complete the analogy given below.
Sweet potato : Modified roots : :
Potato : *X*
- (a) Modified underground leaves
- (b) Buds on leaf margins
- (c) Modified stems
- (d) Modified subaerial stems

2. Which of the following correctly describe the structure given below?

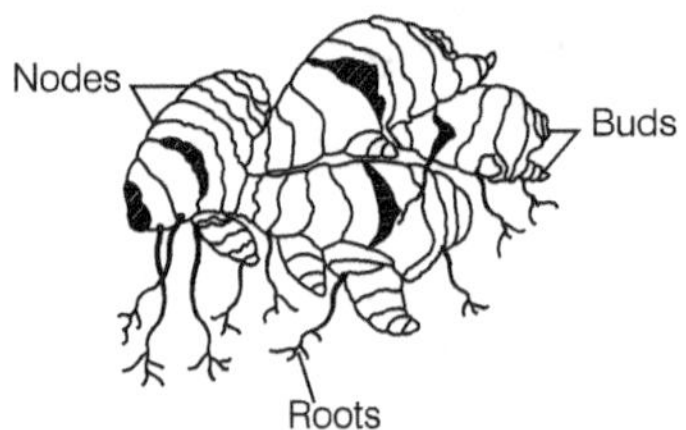

- (a) It is a stem tuber
- (b) It is an underground stem modification called rhizomes
- (c) It represents a bud surrounded by fleshy scale leaves
- (d) It is an outgrowth at base of stem called suckers

3. Riya has the following parts of a rose plant. She wants to grow new rose plants. Which of the following parts she can use? Choose the correct option.

I. A leaf	II. Stem
III. A branch	IV. A flower
V. A bud	VI. Pollen grains

Codes
- (a) II, III and VI
- (b) Only III
- (c) Only II
- (d) II, III, IV and VI

4. Look at the classification chart carefully. Identify *X* and *Y*.

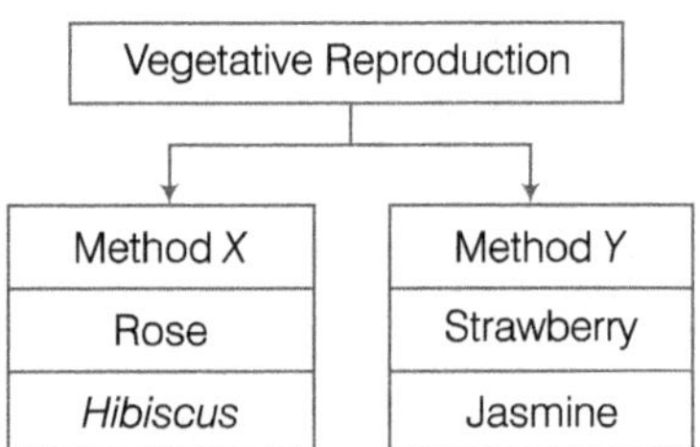

Vegetative Reproduction	
Method *X*	Method *Y*
Rose	Strawberry
Hibiscus	Jasmine

Codes

	X	*Y*
(a)	Cutting	Layering
(b)	Layering	Grafting
(c)	Cutting	Grafting
(d)	Layering	Cutting

5. New plants always grow from seeds. But Shivani has never seen the seeds of a sugarcane or potato plant. Which of the following is a correct explanation for the observation made by Shivani?
- (a) Their seeds cannot grow into new plants.
- (b) These plants do not produce seeds.
- (c) The seeds from these plants are very weak.
- (d) The seeds may carry disease.

6. Refer to the figure given below and select the correct option.

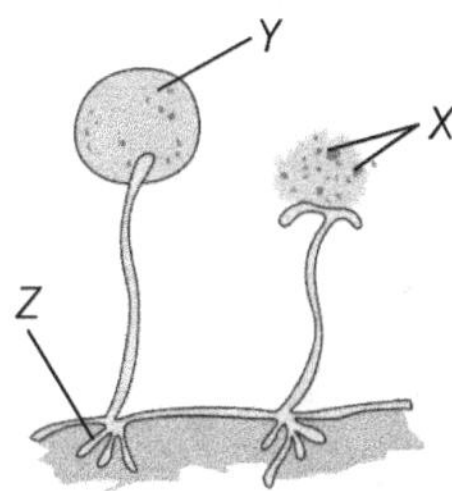

(a) X is the thread-like projections on the plant.
(b) Y is the knob-like structure carrying numerous X.
(c) Z are tiny reproductive bodies of the plant.
(d) X, Y and Z are structures found in sexually reproducing plants.

7. Nividh fills an empty pot with soil. He sowed the budding 'eyes' of a potato in the soil and water it regularly. What do you think Nividh will observe after some days?
(a) Roots can be seen emerging from bulb and shoots from tuber.
(b) Shoot can be seen emerging from bulb and roots from tuber.
(c) Roots and shoots emerge from bulb only.
(d) Roots and shoots emerge from tuber only.

8. Given below are the stages of budding in yeast but are not in correct order.
I. One of the nuclei enters the bud.
II. An outgrowth known as bud forms on the outer surface of a parent cell.
III. The bud cleaves to become a new daughter cell.
IV. The nucleus then divides.
V. A cell wall is formed between the parent cell and the bud.

Which of the following options has the correct sequence of budding in yeast?
(a) I, II, IV, V and III
(b) II, I, V, III and IV
(c) II, IV, I, V and III
(d) IV, I, II, V and III

9. Study the characteristics of a seed shown below.

It is light and has a spongy or fibrous outer coat attached to it which imparts the ability to float.

Based on the above characteristics, how is the seed likely to be dispersed?
(a) By wind   (b) By water
(c) By animals   (d) By splitting

10. The given figure represents the female reproductive parts in a flower

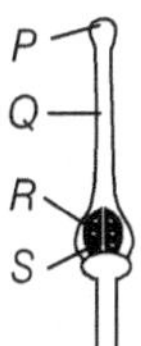

Which part of this flower bears the female gamete?
(a) P (b) Q (c) R (d) S

11. Salma cuts the potato into sections as shown below

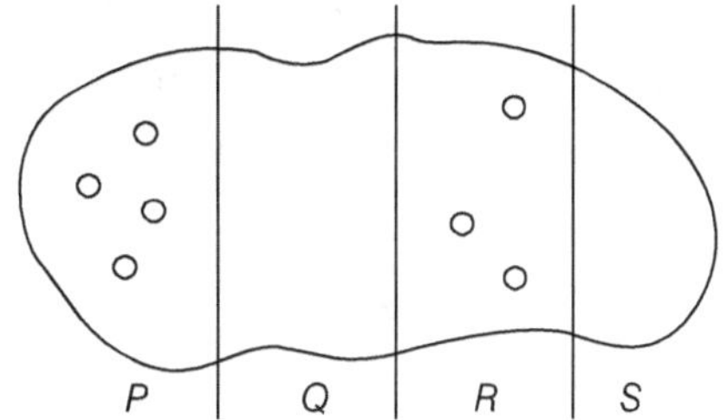

Which sections(s) will not produce new plants?
(a) P only   (b) Q and R
(c) P and R (d) Q and S

12. Observe the flow chart given below and identify *X* and *Y* in it.

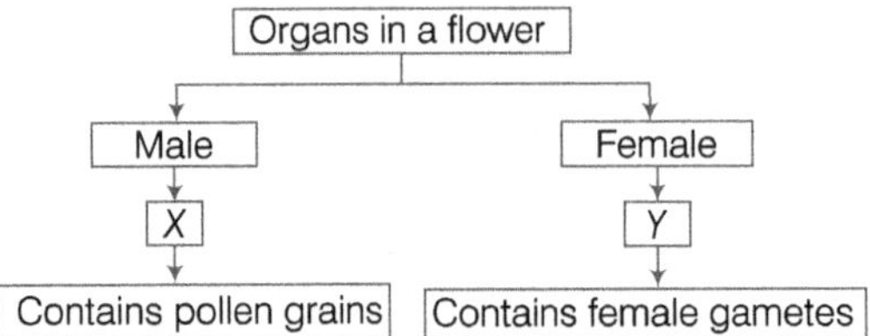

Codes

	X	*Y*
(a)	Stamen	Ovule
(b)	Stigma	Pistil
(c)	Style	Stigma
(d)	Anther	Ovary

13. Which of the following is not a characteristic feature of wind pollinated flower?
(a) Flowers produce huge quantities of pollens.
(b) Petals are brightly coloured and showy.
(c) Pollen grains are light and non-sticky.
(d) Stamen are well-exposed.

14. Which of the following is/are characteristic of insect-pollinated flowers?
A. Nectar is present.

B. Pollen grains are abundant and sticky.
C. Flowers are dull coloured and scentless.
D. Sticky stigmas.
Codes
(a) A and B
(b) B and C
(c) C and D
(d) A, B and D

15. Study the concept map shown below. Which one of these correctly shows *X*, *Y* and *Z* based on the given mapping?

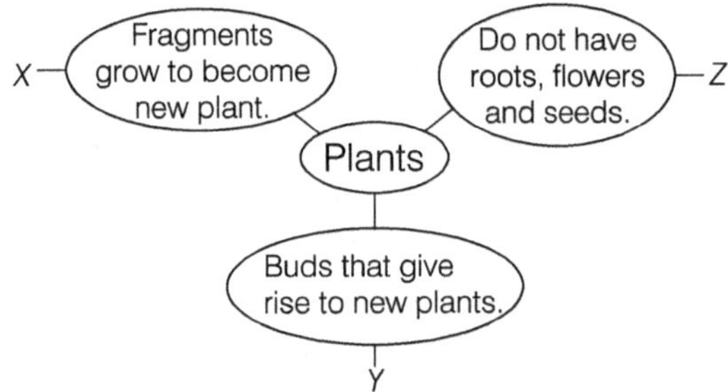

Codes

	X	*Y*	*Z*
(a)	Algae	Turmeric	Moss
(b)	Fern	Potato	Moss
(c)	*Oxalis*	Turmeric	Strawberry
(d)	*Spirogyra*	Algae	*Vallisnera*

2 Marks Questions

16. Observe the figure given below and identify the statement correctly associated with *A*, *B* and *C*.

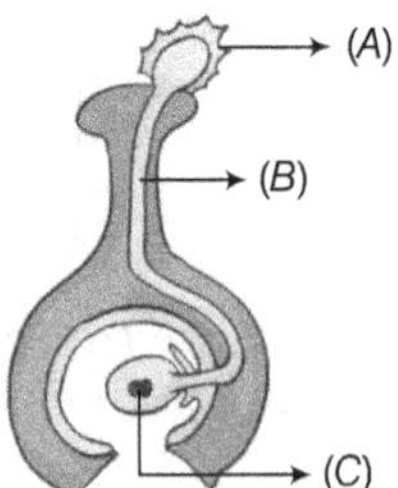

I. *A* is the pollen which carries the male gamete within the flower upon successful pollination.
II. *B* is pollen tube, growing from the pollen through stigma, style and finally to the ovary.
III. *C* is the egg present inside the ovary ready to be fused with male gamete.
IV. *A* and *B* transfer pollen grains during pollination.

Codes
(a) I and II
(b) Only II
(c) II, III and IV
(d) Only IV

17. Refer to the given diagram and choose the correct labelling of P, Q, R and S.

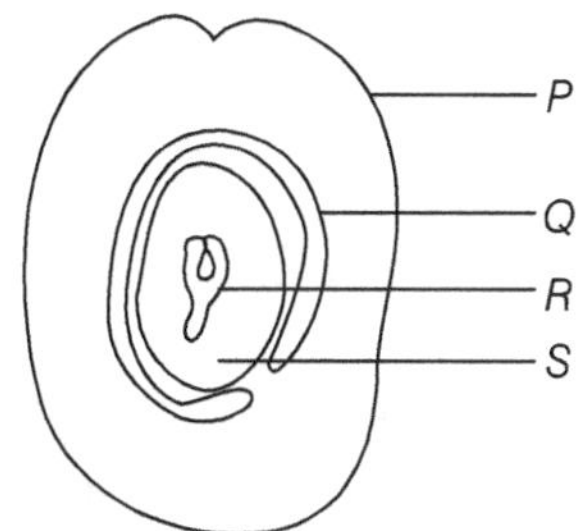

	P	*Q*	*R*	*S*
(a)	Flower	Pistil	Stamen	Petals
(b)	Fruit	Seed coat	Embryo	Endosperm
(c)	Fruit	Embryo	Endosperm	Seed coat
(d)	Sead coat	Endosperm	Fruit	Embryo

18. Observe the given diagrams showing the cross-section of two flowers. Which of the following statements is/are correct regarding them?

Flower *X*   Flower *Y*

I. The flowering plants have developed from seeds.
II. Flower *X* is a female flower and flower *Y* is a bisexual flower.
III. Fertilisation can take place in both flowers.
IV. Their pollen tube keeps on growing till it reaches the sepals.

Codes
(a) Only I
(b) II and III
(c) Only II
(d) II, III and IV

Motion and Time

1 Mark Questions

1. The distance-time graph given below shows a car moving with a constant speed.

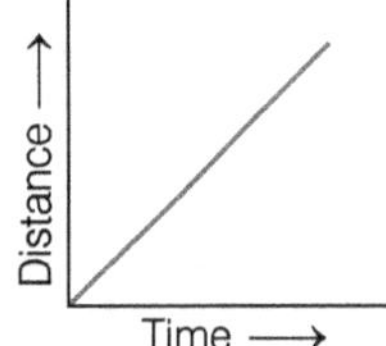

The slope of this graph indicates
(a) time taken by the object
(b) position of the object
(c) speed of the object
(d) distance moved by the object

2. Time taken by a simple pendulum to travel from point A to O is 0.5 s. How much time will it take to complete 10 oscillations?

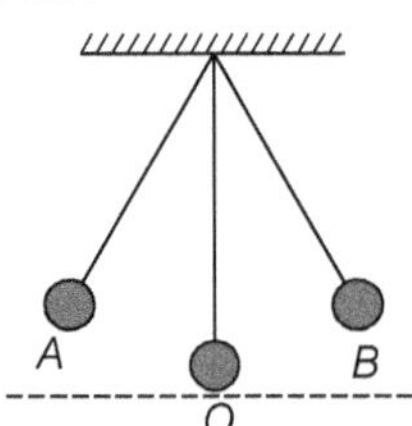

(a) 20 s   (b) 10 s   (c) 5 s   (d) 40 s

3. The radius of Earth is 6371 km approximately. How much distance it travels in completing one rotation?
(a) 40010 km   (b) 400010 km
(c) 4000010 km   (d) 40000 km

4. What is the approximate speed of the Earth, while completing one rotation? [Given, radius of Earth is 6371 km.]
(a) 1500 km/h   (b) 1667 m/s
(c) 1667 km/h   (d) 1500 m/s

5. The distance-time graph of a moving vehicle as shown in figure indicates.

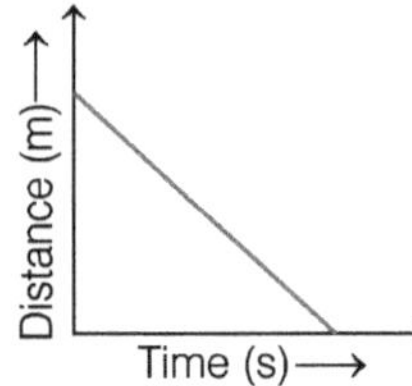

(a) speed of the vehicle is increasing with time
(b) speed of the vehicle is decreasing with time
(c) the final speed of the vehicle is zero
(d) graph is not possible

6. Aman is standing on the platform of a station watching the trains. A train travelling at 30 m/s takes 3 s to pass Aman. What is the length of the train?
(a) 10 m   (b) 60 m
(c) 30 m   (d) 90 m

7. A person follows the following path as shown in the figure given below to reach to his home. What will be the average speed of the person?

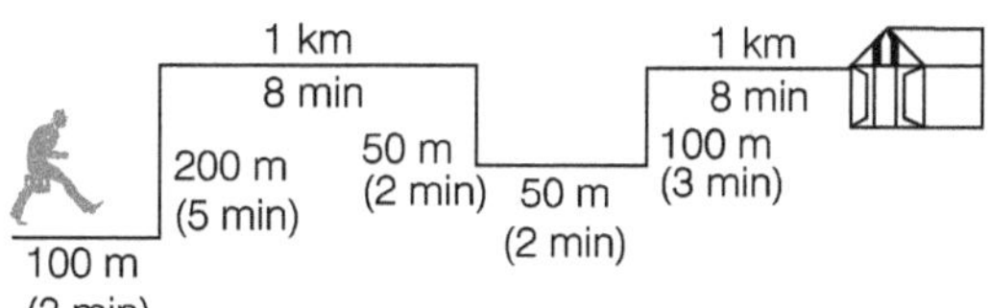

(a) 0.27 m/s   (b) 1.34 m/s
(c) 1.34 m/min   (d) 0.27 m/min

8. Allan is riding a bicycle. In the first hour, he travels at a speed of 10 km/h, in the second hour, he travels at a speed of 15 km/h, in the third hour he travels at a speed of 20 km/h.

   What is the total distance travelled by Allan?

   (a) 15 km   (b) 25 km
   (c) 45 km   (d) 55 km

9. The distance between starting and finishing line in a race is 800 m. In order to set the world record, an athlete needs to finish the race in 15 s. The speed of the athlete will be

   (a) 5.33 ms^{-1} (b) 53.33 ms^{-1}
   (c) 53.33 ms^{-2} (d) 53.33 kms^{-1}

10. While drawing a distance-time graph for a moving bike, the student finds some part of the graph is parallel to the time axis. Which of the following conclusion is correct about this part of the graph?

    (a) This part indicates a uniform speed of the bike.
    (b) The bike travelled the maximum distance in this part of time.
    (c) The bike travelled the minimum distance in this part of time.
    (d) The bike was at rest in this part of time.

11. The motion of a body is depicted graphically as shown in the given figure. Then,

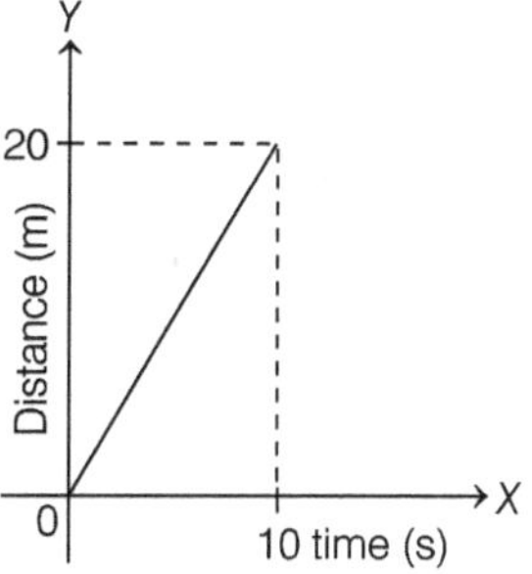

(a) the average speed of the body is 2 ms^{-1}
(b) the average speed of the body is zero
(c) the body changes its direction twice
(d) All of the above

12. Two clocks A and B are shown in figure. Clock A has an hour and a minute hand, whereas clock B has an hour hand, minute hand as well as a second hand. Which of the following statement is correct for these clocks?

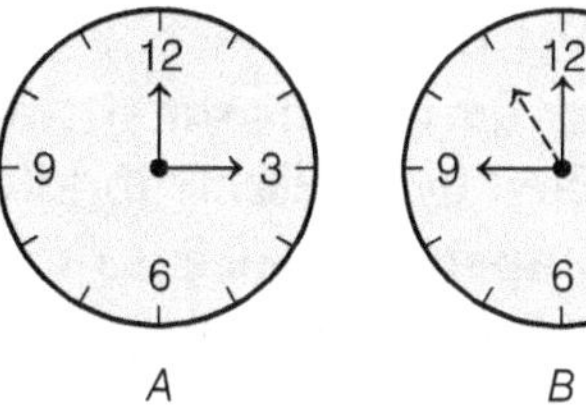

(a) A time interval of 30 s can be measured by clock A
(b) A time interval of 30 s cannot be measured by clock B
(c) Time interval of 5 min can be measured by both A and B
(d) Time interval of 4 min 10 s can be measured by clock A

13. Observe given figure as below:

    The time period of a simple pendulum is the time taken by it to travel from

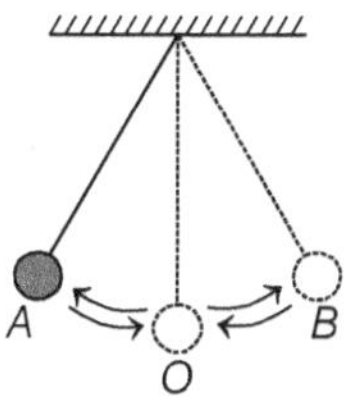

    (a) A to B and back to A
    (b) O to A, A to B and B to A
    (c) B to A, A to B and B to O
    (d) A to B

14. The diagram below shows three pendulums of different height having different weight of bob. Which of the three will have highest time-period?

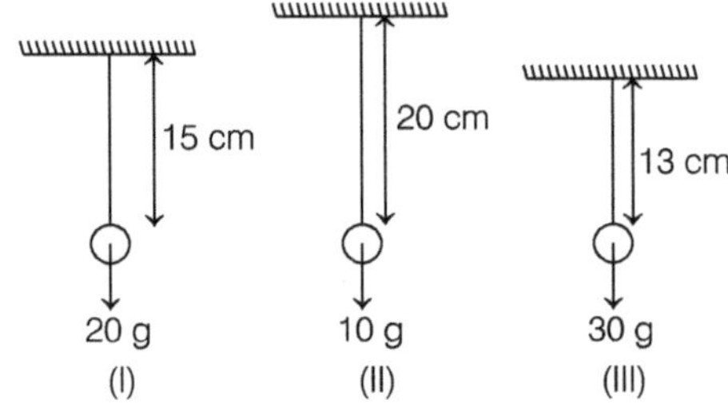

   (a) I   (b) II   (c) III
   (d) All have same time-period

15. Consider the following statements and choose the incorrect ones.

   I. The ratio of speed *versus* distance gives the time taken by an object to cover that distance.
   II. Odometer records the distance travelled by a vehicle in kilometers.
   III. To compare the speeds of a number of objects, units need not be same.

   Codes
   (a) I and II   (b) I and III
   (c) II and III   (d) All of these

16. **Statement I** Circular motion is a non-uniform motion.

   Statement II The speed of a body changes at every point of the curve to be in circular motion.

   Choose the correct option.
   (a) Only statement I is correct.
   (b) Only statement II is correct.
   (c) Both statements are correct.
   (d) Both statements are incorrect.

17. Fill in the blanks with the help of options given in the list.

   (i) non-uniform (ii) uniform
   (iii) kmh^{-1} (iv) periodic
   (v) distance   (vi) odometer
   (vii) ms^{-1} (viii) position
   (ix) speed   (x) rotational

   I. The distance moved by an object per unit time is termed as ....
   II. A moving body changes its .... with the passage of time.
   III. An object moving along a straight line with constant speed is in .... motion.
   IV. The SI unit of speed is ....
   V. The turning of the blades of fan is .... motion.

   Codes

	I	II	III	IV	V
(a)	(ix)	(viii)	(ii)	(vii)	(x)
(b)	(iv)	(i)	(ii)	(iii)	(ix)
(c)	(vi)	(v)	(x)	(viii)	(ix)
(d)	(iii)	(vi)	(ix)	(ii)	(vii)

18. State [T] for True or [F] for False.

   I. The motion of the Earth around the Sun is a uniform motion.
   II. The hands of an athlete, while running a race are in periodic motion.
   III. The speed $36\,kmh^{-1}$ is equivalent to $10\,ms^{-1}$.
   IV. A slower moving object covers a particular distance in shorter time as compared to others.
   V. Distance travelled by an object is the product of speed of the object to the time taken.

   Codes

	I	II	III	IV	V
(a)	F	T	T	F	T
(b)	F	F	T	T	T
(c)	T	T	F	F	T
(d)	T	F	T	T	T

19. Statement I If the speed of a car moving towards North is 60 ms^{-1}, its velocity is 60 ms^{-1} towards the East.

Statement II The velocity of a body is speed in a specified direction.

Choose the correct option.
(a) Only statement I is correct.
(b) Only statement II is correct.
(c) Both statements are correct.
(d) Both statements are incorrect.

20. Which of the following distance-time graphs is not possible?

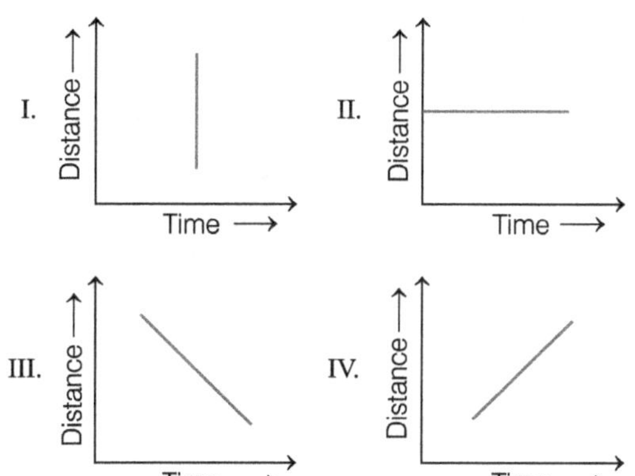

Codes
(a) I and II   (b) I and III
(c) I and IV   (d) II and III

21. Fill in the blanks with the help of options given in the list.
  (i) uniform   (ii) time
 (iii) distance   (iv) non-uniform
  (v) speed   (vi) linear
 (vii) time-period   (viii) periodic
 (ix) parallel.

 I. The slope of distance-time graph gives ....
 II. The time taken by the pendulum to complete one oscillation is called its ....
 III. The time from one sunrise to the next is a .... type of motion.
 IV. The distance-time graph of a body at rest is a straight line parallel to .... axis.
 V. If the distance-time graph of a body is a curved line, it represents body is moving with a .... speed.

Codes

	I	II	III	IV	V
(a)	(v)	(vii)	(viii)	(ii)	(iv)
(b)	(iv)	(i)	(ii)	(iii)	(ix)
(c)	(vi)	(v)	(ii)	(viii)	(ix)
(d)	(iii)	(vi)	(ix)	(ii)	(vii)

22. Statement I If the length of the pendulum is increased, its time-period also increases.

Statement II The time-period of a pendulum is always constant for a particular pendulum.

Choose the correct option.
(a) Only statement I is correct.
(b) Only statement II is correct.
(c) Both statements are correct.
(d) Both statements are incorrect.

2 Marks Questions

23. Rahul is going from the playground back to his home. The distance-time graph of his journey is shown below. Match the statements to the marked positions of the graph correctly.

I. He is going with high speed.

II. He is going back.

III. He takes rest.

IV. He slows down.

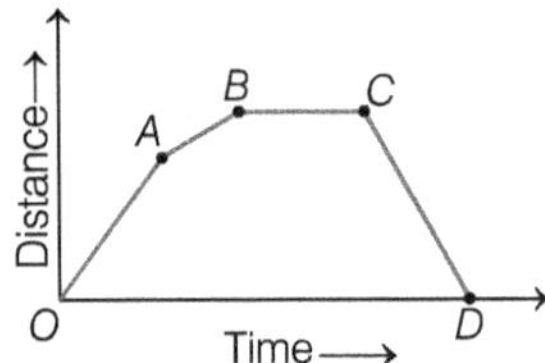

Codes

	I	II	III	IV
(a)	CD	OA	BC	AB
(b)	CD	BC	OA	AB
(c)	OA	CD	BC	AB
(d)	OA	BC	AB	CD

24. A man walks on a straight road from his home to market 2.5 km away with a speed of 5 km/h. Finding the market closed, he instantly turns and walks back home with a speed of 7.5 km/h. The average speed of the man over the interval of time 0 to 40 min is equal to

(a) 5 km/h (b) $\dfrac{25}{4}$ km/h

(c) $\dfrac{30}{4}$ km/h (d) $\dfrac{45}{8}$ km/h

25. Raghav is going to school with his father by car. He decides to note the readings on the odometer of the car after every five minutes till he reaches the school. The given table shows the odometer readings of his journey.

Time (am)	9:30	9:35	9:40	9:45	9:50
Odometer reading (km)	3867	3870	3873	3876	3879

If he left for school at 9 : 30 am, then find the average speed of the car.

(a) 6 m/s (b) 10 m/s

(c) 5 m/s (d) 7 m/s

26. Which of the following options is correct for the object having a straight line motion represented by the graph shown in figure?

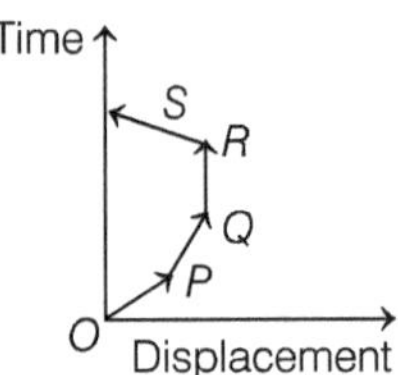

(a) The object moves with constantly increasing velocity from O to P and then it moves with constant velocity.

(b) Velocity of the object increases uniformly.

(c) Average velocity is zero.

(d) The graph shown is impossible.

27. A car at 7:30 am is moving at a constant speed of 4 km/min and an odometer reading recorded is 28568 km. What would be the odometer reading at 9 : 15 am?

(a) 28673 km (b) 28988 km

(c) 29255 km (d) 28568 km

Electric Current and Its Effect

1 Mark Questions

1. Below is a list of materials that can be chosen to replace material X to light up the bulb, EXCEPT ....

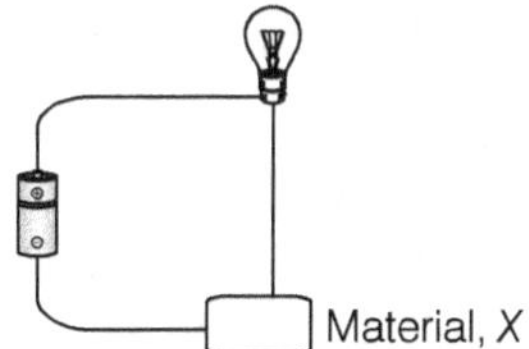

   (a) cotton
   (b) iron
   (c) salt water
   (d) mercury

2. Which of the following statement is true in context with the circuit given below?

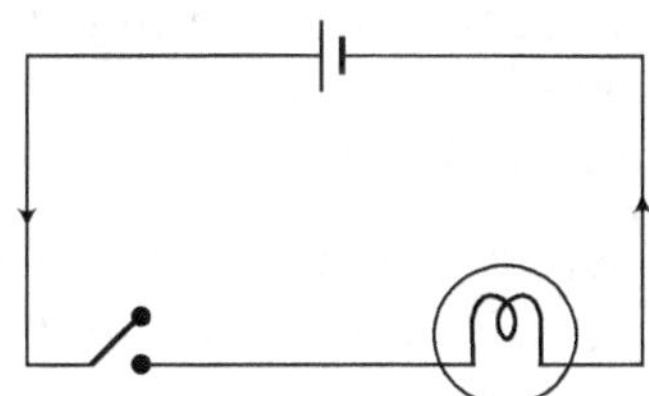

   (a) It is a complete circuit so current will flow through it
   (b) Switch is open, so bulb cannot glow
   (c) Wire is broken
   (d) The direction of flow of current is not correct

3. Manoj set up an electrical circuit as shown below.

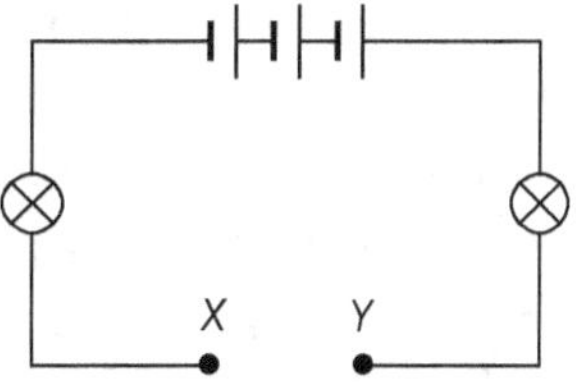

   He wants to be able to control the brightness of both bulbs using a dimmer. Which of the following electrical devices should he connect between X and Y?

   (a) —Ⓐ—
   (b) —Ⓥ—
   (c) —▭—
   (d) —▱—

4. A toy car needs a 12 V battery for its operation. How many cells of 1.5 V are required to provide the needed potential difference?

   (a) 7
   (b) 8
   (c) 6
   (d) 9

54   **SCIENCE OLYMPIAD** Class VII

5. Electric circuits consisting of a bulb (or bulbs), a key and a cell are shown below. In which of the following circuits the bulb will glow?

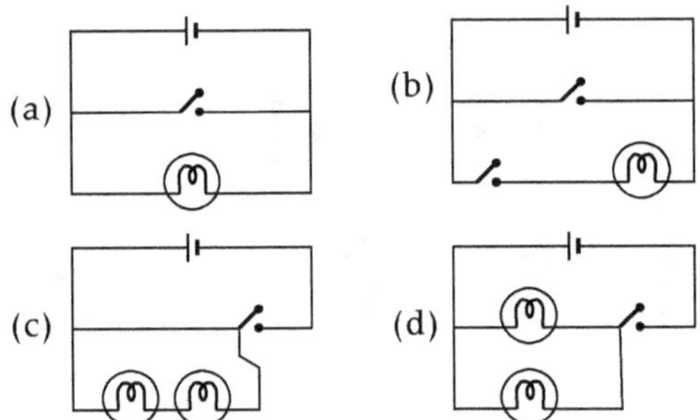

6. Which of the following does not work on the heating effect of current?
(a) Electric bulb
(b) Electric fuse
(c) Miniature circuit breaker (MCB)
(d) Immersion rod

7. When an electric current is flows through a conductor, it produces heat. The amount of heat produced in a heating element depends on
(a) its length
(b) area of cross-section
(c) nature of material
(d) All of the above

8. Fuse wires are made from special materials that melt quickly and break when large electric currents are passed through them. They are made up of which of the following alloy?
(a) Nichrome   (b) Tin-lead
(c) Magno-chrome (d) Chrome-lead

9. An arrangement of cell, bulb and connecting wires to glow bulb is shown as below.

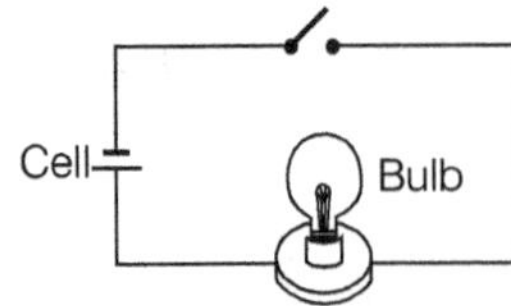

When key is closed, electric current passes through the filament of bulb and it gives off.
(a) Heat and sound
(b) Sound and magnetism
(c) Heat and light
(d) Sound and light

10. What is the name given to the coil of an electromagnet?
(a) Magnetic coil   (b) Key
(c) Solenoid   (d) Element

11. An electromagnet is operated on which type of power supply?
(a) Alternating current (AC)
(b) Direct current (DC)
(c) Either (a) or (b)
(d) Neither (a) nor (b)

12. The strength of an electromagnet depend upon
(a) number of turns in the coil
(b) current passing through the coil
(c) nature of core material
(d) All of the above

13. An electromagnet is a temporary magnet, whose strength can be changed. It works only when current is
(a) allowed to flow through it
(b) not allowed to flow through it
(c) allowed and then stopped
(d) None of the above

14. What will happen if electromagnet is replaced with a bar magnet?
(a) The circuit is not correct
(b) The bell will ring continuously even without circuit being complete
(c) The bell will not ring when current is passed through it
(d) There will be no change and bar magnet will work just like the electromagnet

15. Identify the figure given as below. On which principle does it work?

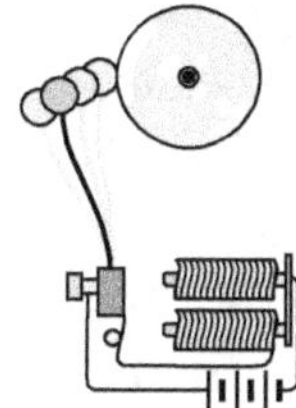

(a) Electromagnet, magnetic effect of current
(b) Electric bell, heating effect of current
(c) Electric bell, magnetic effect of current
(d) Loudspeaker, magnetic effect of current

16. Which of the following circuit shows the correct way of connecting an ammeter and a voltmeter?

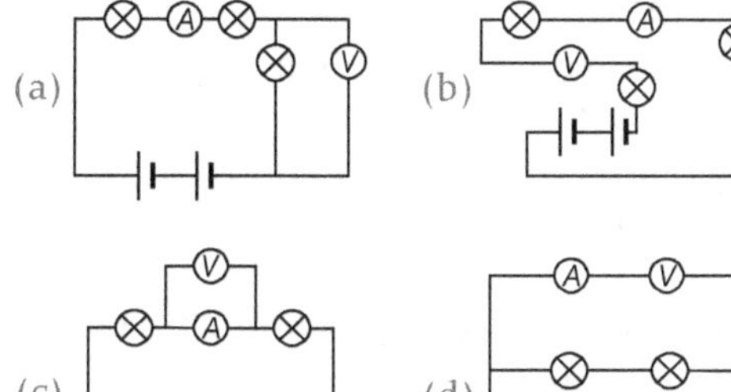

17. When a switch is in OFF position, then
  I. current starting from the positive terminal of the cell stops at the switch.
  II. circuit is open.
  III. no current flows through it.
  IV. current flows after some time.
  Choose the combination of correct answer from the following.
  (a) Only IV
  (b) Both I and II
  (c) Both II and III
  (d) All of the above

18. Fill in the blanks with the help of options given in the box.
   (i) magnet   (ii) MCB
  (iii) magnetic field   (iv) current
   (v) electric bell   (vi) coil
  (vii) electromagnet   (viii) solenoid
   I. Current flowing in a wire gives rise to .... around it.
   II. The magnet made by using electric current is called ....
   III. A current carrying coil of an insulated wire wrapped around a piece of iron is called ....
   IV. .... works on the magnetic effect of current.
   V. The safety device based on magnetic effect of current is called ....

Codes
         I   II   III   IV   V
  (a) (iii)(vii)(viii)(v) (ii)
  (b) (ii) (vii)(iv) (iii) (v)
  (c) (v) (i) (ii)(viii)(iii)
  (d) (viii) (i)(v) (ii) (vi)

19. Match the given matrix.

A. Bulb	1. —
B. Ammeter	2. —(V)—
C. Key	3. —(A)—
D. Cell	4. —(•)—
E. Voltmeter	5. —⌒—
	6. —|⊢—

Codes
        A   B   C   D   E
  (a) 5   3   1,4   6   2
  (b) 5   3   1,2   6   4
  (c) 5   2   4   6   3,1
  (d) 5   1   4   2,6   3

20. State [T] for True or [F] for False.
    I. A key or switch in circuit can be placed anywhere in the circuit.
    II. To make a battery of two cells, the longer line is connected to the longer line of another cell.
    III. Household water is a good conductor of electricity.
    IV. The bulb glows in the circuit only when key is in open position.
    V. The SI unit of electric current is ampere.

    Codes

	I	II	III	IV	V
(a)	T	F	T	T	T
(b)	T	F	T	F	T
(c)	T	T	T	F	F
(d)	F	F	T	F	T

21. Consider the following statements and choose the incorrect one.
    I. If the current passing through the conductor is increased, heat produced will also increase.
    II. If resistance of wire is increased, heat produced in it will decrease.
    III. Heating element is made up of tungsten wire.

    Codes
    (a) I and II   (b) II and III
    (c) I and III   (d) All of these

22. Which of the following are not based on the magnetic effect of electric current?
    I. CFL   II. Loudspeaker
    III. Electric bell   IV. Electric motor

    Codes
    (a) Only I   (b) I and II
    (c) I and III   (d) Only IV

23. Complete the following paragraph using the words given in options below:
    It was observed by Oersted that when a .... compass is brought near a current carrying .... the needle of the compass gets deflected in the .... of flow of electricity.
    (a) electromagnets, direction, core
    (b) magnetic, conductor, direction
    (c) magnetic, direction, core
    (d) electromagnets, core, direction

24. The element of a heating appliance is made of an alloy nichrome but not of tungsten. This is so, because
    (a) tungsten catches fire in presence of air but nichrome do not
    (b) tungsten is not a good conductor of electricity
    (c) colour of nichrome makes it possible to become red hot and cause heating effect
    (d) All of the above

25. Which of the following statements are correct?
    I. Fuse works on heating effect of electric current.
    II. Electromagnets are used in many devices such as electric bell, cranes, etc.
    III. Fuses have replaced MCBs in modern buildings.
    IV. An electromagnet does not attract safety pins.

    Codes
    (a) I and II   (b) Only II
    (c) I and III   (d) Only IV

26. Which of the following statements are incorrect?
    I. Fuse is a safety device.
    II. Modern houses use Miniature Circuit Breakers.
    III. MCB needs to be replaced everytime a heavy electric current passes through it.
    IV. MCB serves the same purpose as a CFL.

    Codes
    (a) I and II   (b) Only II
    (c) III and IV   (d) Only III

2 Marks Questions

27. Sammy designed a doorbell as shown below.

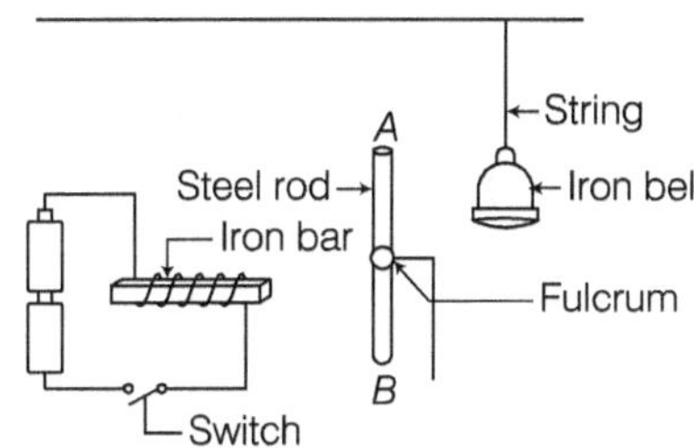

The energy changes that take place in the electric bell are

(a) kinetic → electrical → magnetic → sound

(b) electrical → kinetic → magnetic → sound

(c) electrical → magnetic → kinetic → sound

(d) electrical → chemical → magnetic → sound

28. When the switch of an electric bell is pushed, then

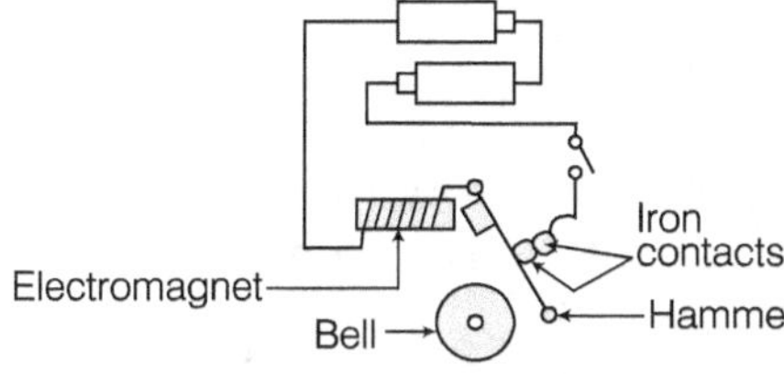

(a) flow of the current stops through the electromagnet in the bell

(b) a current starts to flow through the electromagnet

(c) voltage decreases in the current flowing through the electromagnet

(d) None of the above

29.

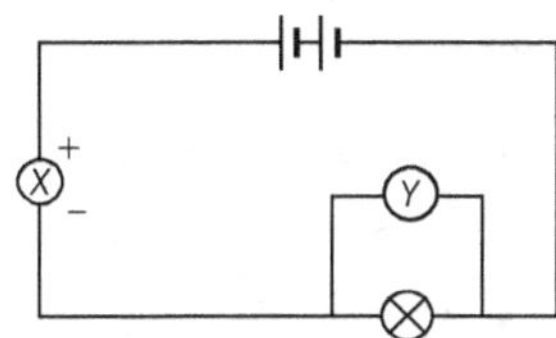

Which of the following statements about the above circuit is correct?

(a) Instrument X measures the voltage as the current flows through the circuit

(b) Instrument X measures the voltage of the light bulb

(c) Instrument Y measures the voltage of the light bulb

(d) Instrument Y measures the amount of current flowing through the circuit

30. State [T] for True or [F] for False.

I. A fuse is used to save energy in electric circuits.

II. Fuse wire is made up of an alloy of lead and copper which are in different proportions.

III. Electric iron works on heating effect of current.

IV. Connecting many devices to a single socket leads to short-circuit.

V. If live wire comes in contact with neutral wire, it leads to short-circuit.

Codes

	I	II	III	IV	V
(a)	T	F	T	T	T
(b)	T	T	F	F	T
(c)	T	T	T	F	F
(d)	F	F	T	T	T

31. Match the given matrix.

A.	Fuse	1.	Nichrome
B.	Filament	2.	Live and neutral wire comes in direct contact
C.	Element	3.	Large current drawn from same socket
D.	Overloading	4.	High resistance and low melting point
E.	Short-circuit	5.	Tungsten

Codes

	A	B	C	D	E
(a)	4	5	1	3	2
(b)	4	1	5	3	2
(c)	4	1	5	2	3
(d)	4	5	1	2	3

Light

1 Mark Questions

1. The term lateral inversion refers to
   (a) appearance of inverted images
   (b) appearance of erect images
   (c) appearance of left side of object on right side of image and *vice-versa*
   (d) appearance of left side of object on left side of image and *vice-versa*

2. The letter G is placed in front of a plane mirror. How would its image look like when seen in the mirror?

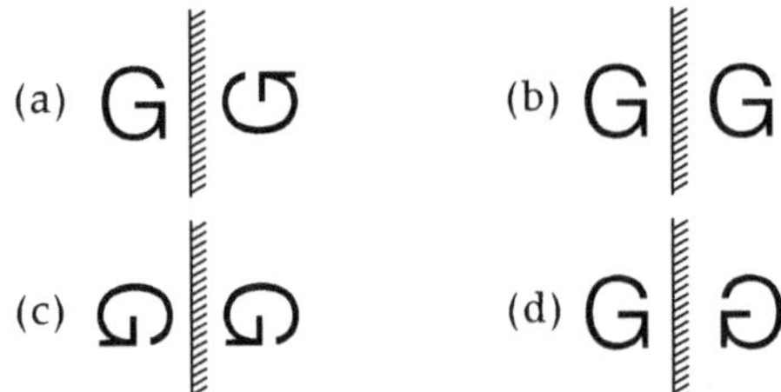

3. Geeta stood 4 m away from a plane mirror, then she moved again 1 m away. Now, the distance between her and image is
   (a) 5 m   (b) 6 m
   (c) 8 m   (d) 10 m

4. I am a spherical mirror. Unlike my other companion. I can form real and inverted as well virtual and erect images. Dentists rely on me to cure their patients. Who am I?
   (a) Convex mirror   (b) Plane mirror
   (c) Concave mirror (d) Either (a) or (c)

5. Rama takes a prism to see the dispersion of white light through it. She observes when a ray of light passes through prism,
   (a) the deviation of red light is maximum
   (b) the deviation of violet light is maximum
   (c) the deviation of blue light is maximum
   (d) All rays deviate equally

6. Sir Newton discovered me using a simple experiment of glass prism. The secret of rainbow formation was revealed when I came into existence. Who am I?
   (a) Reflection   (b) Refraction
   (c) Dispersion   (d) Medium

7. I always form virtual, erect and diminished image. If you want to know who I am just observe an air bubble in water, then
   (a) spherical lens   (b) concave lens
   (c) convex lens   (d) cylindrical lens

8. The distance between an object and a convex lens is changing. The size of the image formed has been observed to be decreasing. In which direction does the object moving with respect to lens?

(a) Towards the lens
(b) Away from the lens
(c) Initially towards and then away from the lens
(d) Initially away from the lens and then towards the lens

9. The given figures show the path of light through two lenses *A* and *B* represented by rectangular boxes. The nature of lenses *A* and *B* are

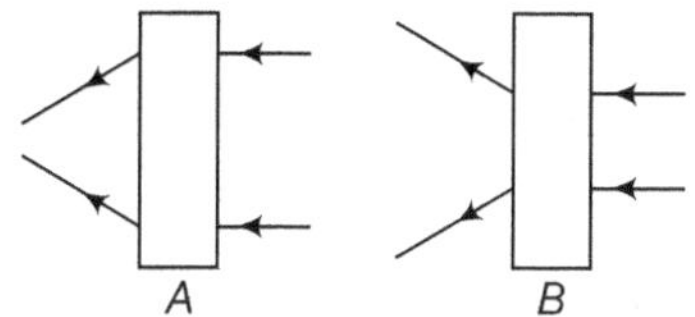

(a) *A* convex, *B* concave
(b) *A* concave, *B* convex
(c) *A* concave, *B* concave
(d) *A* convex, *B* convex

10. During an experiment, a lens *X* was kept on a table and a lighted candle was placed at a distance from the focus. The image was found to be real, inverted and diminished. When the candle was moved closer to the lens, the size of the image was found to be increasing. The lens *X* is
(a) concave lens   (b) convex lens
(c) prism   (d) Both (a) and (b)

11. The image formed by certain lens is always virtual, erect and smaller in size for an object kept at different positions in front of it. The lens must be
(a) convex lens
(b) concave lens
(c) plano-convex lens
(d) Either (a) or (b)

12. Reflection of light is the change in direction of light by a mirror or any shiny surface that acts as a mirror. Reena held a stainless steel spoon to see her reflection. She saw that her reflection was
(a) inverted on the outer side of the spoon
(b) erect on the inner side of the spoon
(c) erect on the outer side of the spoon
(d) inverted on the inner side of the spoon

13. I am a spherical mirror. My bulging out face performs the reflection. I am used as a rear view mirror in vehicles. I give a wide field of view. Who am I?
(a) Spherical mirror (b) Convex mirror
(c) Plane mirror   (d) Concave mirror

14. Boojho and Paheli were given one mirror each by their teacher. Boojho found his image to be erect and of the same size whereas Paheli found her image erect and smaller in size. This means that the mirrors of Boojho and Paheli are respectively
(a) plane mirror and concave mirror
(b) concave mirror and convex mirror
(c) plane mirror and convex mirror
(d) convex mirror and plane mirror

15. I. The incident ray, reflected ray and normal ray never lies on the same plane.
II. The angle made by the incident ray with the plane of mirror is equal to the angle made by reflected ray with the plane of mirror.
III. The angle made by incident ray with the normal is equal to the angle made by reflected ray with the normal.

Consider the following statement and choose the incorrect one.
Codes
(a) I and II   (b) II and III
(c) I and III   (d) All are incorrect

16. I. When an object is placed close to a concave mirror, the image will be virtual, erect and magnified.

II. Convex mirrors always form virtual, erect and diminished images.

III. Lateral inversion is possible only with convex mirrors.

Consider the following statement and choose the incorrect one.

Codes
(a) Only III
(b) II and III
(c) I and III
(d) All are correct

17. Fill in the blanks with the help of options given in the box.

(i) Non-luminous (ii) virtual
(iii) plane   (iv) convex
(v) real   (vi) concave
(vii) luminous   (viii) reflection
(ix) diffraction   (x) dispersion

I. ....images are the one which can be taken on screen.

II. The image formed in a plane mirror is ....

III. Dentists use .... mirrors to see the infected tooth.

IV. A periscope works on the principle of .... of light.

V. .... bodies emit their own light.

Codes

	I	II	III	IV	V
(a)	(v)	(ii)	(vi)	(viii)	(vii)
(b)	(vii)	(viii)	(ix)	(ii)	(v)
(c)	(v)	(x)	(iii)	(vii)	(ix)
(d)	(i)	(iv)	(iii)	(ix)	(vii)

18. In which type of lens, images formed are always diminished?
(a) Concave lens   (b) Convex lens
(c) Spherical lens   (d) Plane lens

19. I. Convex lens is thicker at the edges and thinner in the middle.

II. Concave lens is thinner in the middle and thicker at the edges.

III. Convex lens is also known as converging lens.

IV. Concave lens is also known as converging lens.

Read the above statements and choose the incorrect one.

Codes
(a) I and III   (b) II and III
(c) I and IV   (d) II and IV

20. **Statement I** Lenses work on the refraction of light.

Statement II Lenses are transparent, so light can pass through them.

Choose the correct option.
(a) Only statement I is correct.
(b) Only statement II is correct.
(c) Both statements are correct.
(d) Both statements are incorrect.

21. **Statement I** A rainbow is formed when white light is incident on raindrops.

Statement II White light contains seven colours which undergoes dispersion inside a raindrop.

Choose the correct option.
(a) Only statement I is correct.
(b) Only statement II is correct.
(c) Both statements are correct.
(d) Both statements are incorrect.

22. State [T] for True or [F] for False.

I. The image in a concave lens is always smaller than the object.

II. Convex lens gives a wide field of view.

III. It is possible to recombine the lights of seven colours to obtain white light.

IV. Infrared rays are responsible to give the heating effect in light.

V. Lenses work on the reflection of light bouncing from them.

Codes

	I	II	III	IV	V
(a)	T	F	T	T	F
(b)	T	T	F	F	T
(c)	T	T	T	F	F
(d)	F	F	T	F	T

23. Match the given matrix.

A.	Lens	1.	Dispersion
B.	Convex lens	2.	Divergent
C.	Concave lens	3.	Seven colours
D.	Prism	4.	Refraction
E.	White light	5.	Convergent

Codes

	A	B	C	D	E
(a)	4	2	5	3	1
(b)	4	2	5	1	3
(c)	4	5	2	1	3
(d)	4	5	2	3	1

2 Marks Questions

24. State [T] for True and [F] for False.

I. The distance of the object from the mirror is equal to the distance of the image from the mirror in case of a plane mirror.

II. Like plane mirror, spherical mirrors also produce laterally inverted images.

III. The angle between the incident ray and reflected ray is the angle of reflection.

IV. Reflection is the bouncing back of light from a surface.

V. The nature of images formed by a concave mirror varies with the position of the object.

Codes

	I	II	III	IV	V
(a)	T	F	F	T	T
(b)	T	T	F	F	T
(c)	T	T	T	F	F
(d)	F	F	T	F	T

25. Fill in the blanks with the help of options given in the list.

(i) concave   (ii) diverging
(iii) spectrum   (iv) convex
(v) reflection   (vi) converging
(vii) seven   (viii) refraction
(ix) dispersion   (x) real

I. A magnifying glass is a .... lens used to magnify small objects.

II. Convex lens is also known as .... lens.

III. Splitting of light into constituent colours is called ....

IV. A prism splits sunlight into .... colours.

V. The band of seven colours of white light is called ....

Codes

	I	II	III	IV	V
(a)	(iv)	(vi)	(ix)	(vii)	(iii)
(b)	(vii)	(viii)	(ix)	(ii)	(v)
(c)	(v)	(x)	(iii)	(vii)	(ix)
(d)	(i)	(iv)	(iii)	(ix)	(vii)

26. Match the given matrix with the help of adjust figure.

p.	Angle of incidence	A
q.	Normal	B
r.	Reflected ray	C
s.	Angle of reflection	D
t.	Incident ray	E
u.	Spherical mirror	F
v	Plane mirror	

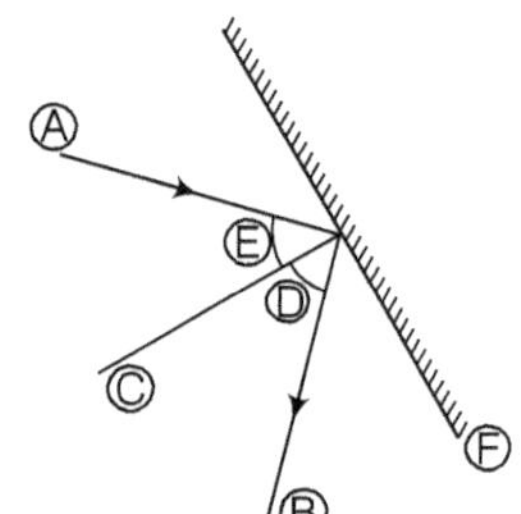

Codes

	A	B	C	D	E	F
(a)	t	q	r	p	s	v
(b)	t	r	q	s	p	v
(c)	t	r	q	p	s	u
(d)	t	r	q	p	s	v

27. A wall separates a person from a ball but he is still able to see it.

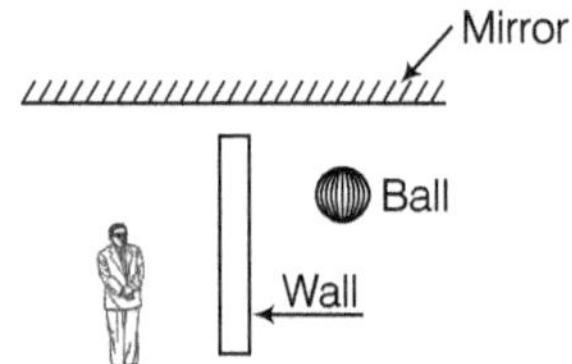

Which one of the following shows how this was possible?

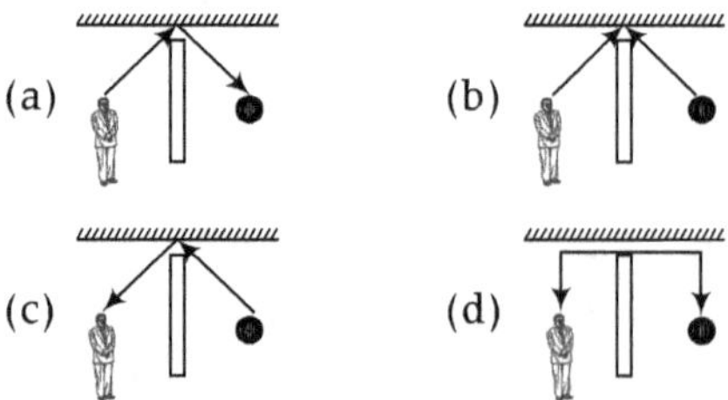

28. An object O is placed between two plane mirrors as shown below. At which position will an image not be seen?

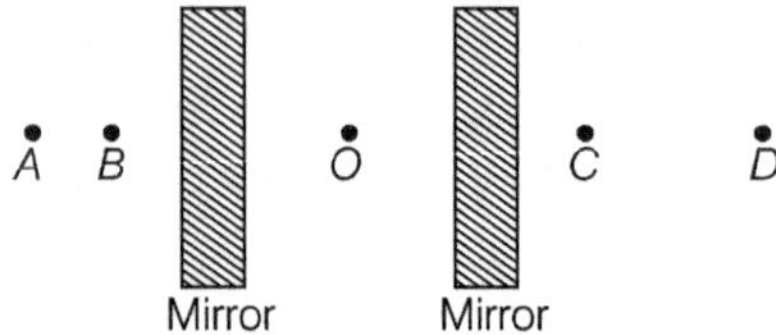

(a) Only A (b) Both B and C
(c) Only C (d) Only D

29. Stained glass can be seen in windows of many medieval buildings throughout Europe. It is a colourful art form and is best viewed when light is passing through it. How are we able to see the different colours of the glass?

(a) There must be reflection and refraction of the sun's rays inside the raindrops
(b) Light is refracted into our eyes
(c) Light is reflected into our eyes
(d) When light passes through the coloured glass, only light rays of that colour enter our eyes

30. Complete the following passage using hints given as below:

A .... causes the .... light to get dispersed into its constituent components. When a ray ....
into the prism, it undergoes ....
twice. It is because of its non-parallel refracting sides that cause ....

(a) prism, refraction, dispersion, white, passes
(b) white, prism, passes, dispersion, refraction
(c) refraction, dispersion, prism, white, dispersion
(d) prism, white, passes, refraction, dispersion

Natural Resources and Their Conservation

1 Mark Questions

1. Soil has four distinct layers in its profile, among them the organic matter is present in
(a) *A*-horizon   (b) *C*-horizon
(c) *B*-horizon   (d) *R*-horizon

2. Unweathered rocks in a soil profile are identified as
(a) substratum   (b) top soil
(c) bedrock   (d) subsoil

3. Select the option which identifies the pollutants of soil from the table given below

  I. Chemicals   II. Plastic bags
III. Dried leaves   IV. Plastic bottle
 V. Paper bags
Codes
(a) I, II and IV   (b) III and V
(c) I, III and V   (d) All of these

4. Arrange the following soil types according to their water holding capacity from highest to lowest.
(a) sandy > loamy > clayey
(b) loamy > sandy > clayey
(c) clayey > loamy > sandy
(d) sandy > clayey > loamy

5. Sandy soil is so well aerated because of the
(a) presence of water in large spaces of soil
(b) large spaces between soil particles
(c) air present in large spaces between soil particles
(d) finer soil particles present close together

6. The rate of percolation for a 500 mL soil sample which took 30 minutes to percolate will be approx.
(a) 16.6
(b) 39
(c) 24
(d) 20.4

7. Akriti heard from her neighbours that 7-10 days after good rainfall, the level of water in ponds rises quite high.

Which type of soil allows the surface water to percolate below the ground at a faster rate?
(a) Sandy loamy soil
(b) Clayey soil
(c) Loamy-clayey
(d) Sandy soil

8. In the grit and sand removal tank of sewage treatment plants, what type of impurities are segregated?
  (a) Solid and heavy objects which settle at bottom.
  (b) Floatable materials.
  (c) Bacteria and other microbes.
  (d) Inorganic impurities.

9. Untreated human excreta is considered as a health hazard. This is because
  (a) it contains disease causing microbes
  (b) it cannot be digested by anaerobic bacteria
  (c) it can clog the sewage system within the houses.
  (d) it is a waste matter discharged from human bodies.

10. The soil where clay content is higher, are often water logged. This is a disadvantage for plants growing in the soil because
  (a) air occupies the space between soil particles
  (b) water occupies the space between soil particles
  (c) the level of ground water increases tremendously
  (d) All of the above

11. Read the following statements given below.
  I. Spraying fertilisers on crops.
  II. Excreting in open area.
  III. Disposal of waste in sewers.
  IV. Constructing more pukka floor.
  Select the activities that will helps in reducing the level of water pollution.
  Codes
  (a) I and II
  (b) All of these except IV
  (c) Only III
  (d) II and III

12. Water circulates in three forms in the nature, i.e. solid, liquid and gas. In the figure given below identify the form of water at places labelled P and Q.

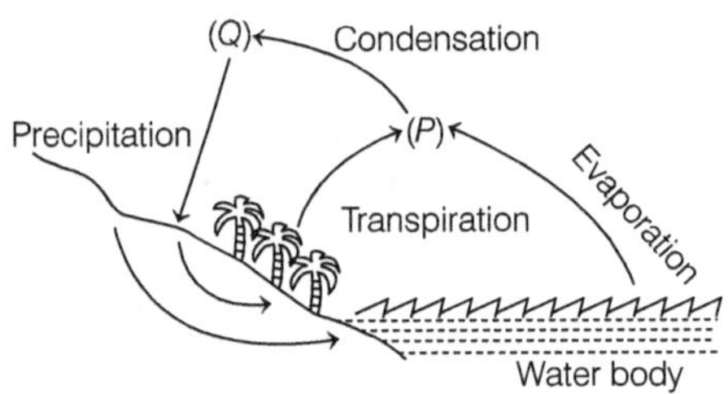

  (a) P-Vapour, Q-Liquid
  (b) P-Liquid, Q-Vapour
  (c) P-Vapour, Q-Gas
  (d) P-Solid, Q-Liquid

13. Given below are statements associated with ozone.
  I. Essential for breathing in humans.
  II. Absorb UV rays.
  III. Used for disinfecting water.
  IV. Used as fertilisers.
  Which of the following statements are correct?
  Codes
  (a) I and II
  (b) III and IV
  (c) I and IV
  (d) II and III

14. Read the statements given below and select the correct option.

  Statement I Wheat grows well in clayey and loamy soil as they are good at retaining water.

  Statement II For cotton, soil rich in clay and humus with good water retention is suitable.
  (a) Statement I is correct, but II is incorrect.
  (b) Statement I is incorrect, but II is correct.
  (c) Both statements are correct.
  (d) Both statements are incorrect.

15. 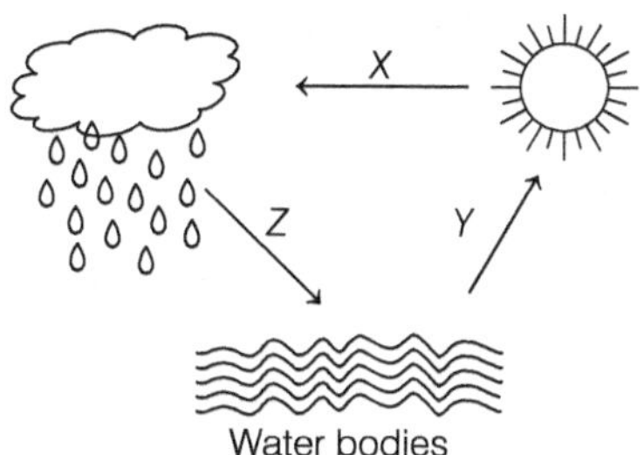

In the diagram above which process is indicated by *Y*?
(a) Collection   (b) Evaporation
(c) Condensation   (d) Precipitation

16. Of all the water that is present on the Earth, humans can use only about three tenths percent of it.

This readily usable water is found in how many of the given sources?

ground water, oceans, aquifers, rivers, freshwater lakes, ice caps and glaciers.
(a) 4   (b) 6   (c) 3   (d) 5

17. Given below are the sources of water that is available to humans. Which of the following is a correct match to its description?

(a)   Infiltration   Water available in moist soil.

(b)   Groundwater   Water found below the water table.

(c)   Bawris   Seeping of water into the ground.

(d)   Aquifer   Rainwater that has yet not seeped into the ground.

18. A sewage treatment plant involves following components during the processing of waste water.

I. Aeration tank.

II. Grit and sand removal tank.

III. Bar screen.

IV. Sedimentation tank.

V. Sludge digester.

The correct arrangement of the above steps as in sewage treatment plants is given by which option?
(a) I → II → IV → III and V
(b) IV → V → I → II and III
(c) III → II → IV → I and V
(d) II → V → III → IV and I

2 Marks Questions

19. The figure given below shows the process involved in the water cycle.

I. Due to heat of the Sun, this process collects water from surface of the Earth as vapours.

II. The water present below the Earth's surface.

III. On cooling at greater heights, the vapour forms clouds through this process.

IV. Water flow over the land as run off in form of rain, snow, hail, etc.

Match the numbers given in the figure to identify the processes involved in statements I-IV

Codes

	I	II	III	IV
(a)	1	2	3	5
(b)	2	1	3	6
(c)	5	4	1	2
(d)	3	5	6	1

20. Aditya placed a handful of soil in beaker with 500 mL water. After leaving the beaker untouched for a while he observed the order in which different components of soil segregated.

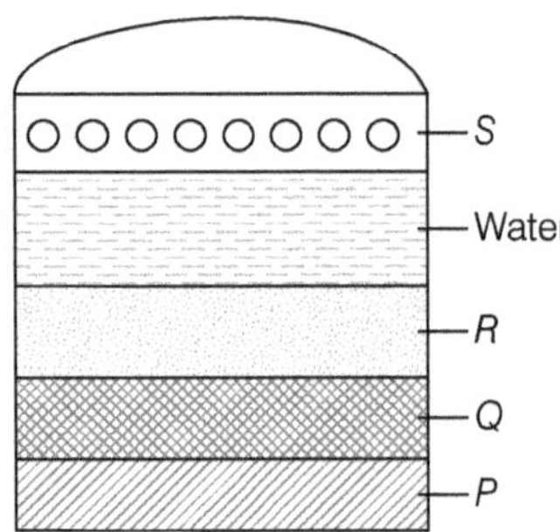

Select the option which identifies the labels correctly w.r.t the figure.

(a) *P* is gravel present in large amounts in top soil

(b) *Q* is slit, which makes the soil heavy and cause water logging

(c) *R* is clay whose particles are compactly arranged and have little air

(d) *S* is humus which degrades the soil quality

21. Read the following statements. Select the option which correctly identifies each of these statements as True (T) and False (F).

I. In clayey soil, proportion of fine and large particles is equal.

II. Erosion of soil is more severe in areas with little vegetation.

III. Use of plastics should be banned to avoid soil pollution.

IV. Desalination is an effect of soil erosion.

Codes

	I	II	III	IV
(a)	T	F	T	F
(b)	F	T	T	F
(c)	T	F	F	T
(d)	F	T	F	F

22. The figure given below represents a technique used in agricultural process.

I. This method helps in economical irrigation of agricultural fields.

II. It is known as terrace farming practiced in mountain regions.

III. This is known as barwris used to recharge groundwater level.

Select the option which identifies the statement that are correct w.r.t the figure.

Codes

(a) I and III   (b) Only I

(c) Only II   (d) Only III

Chapter 16

Forests

1 Mark Questions

1. The destruction of a forest is ultimately the destruction of
   (a) ecosystem
   (b) flora of the forest
   (c) fauna of the region
   (d) soil

2. Among the environment friendly activities mentioned below which will help in conservation of forests?
   (a) Recycling plastic bags
   (b) Recycling jute bags
   (c) Recycling paper bags
   (d) Recycling of metal containers

3. Forests purify the air in the atmosphere. If forests disappear then the
   (a) CO_2 level will decrease
   (b) O_2 level will increase
   (c) O_2 and CO_2 remain balanced
   (d) CO_2 level will increase

4. Which of the following is not produced by the action of decomposers on the dead remains of plants and animals?
   (a) Carbon dioxide
   (b) Oxygen
   (c) Water
   (d) Nutrients

5. I am the thickest layer in a forest. Much of the sunlight and rain can't reach past my thick foliage.
   Which layer am I?
   (a) Forest floor   (b) Understory
   (c) Canopy   (d) Emergent layer

6. In a food chain, which of the following pairs of organism will be identified as primary consumers?
   (a) Deer, lion, man
   (b) Goat, rabbit, horses
   (c) Deer, hawk, snake
   (d) Fungi, cows, insects

7. Which of the following depicts a food chain that can occur in a forest ecosystem?
   (a) Grass → Deer → Lion
   (b) Bushes → Cat → Hawk
   (c) Dog → Hen → Snake
   (d) Bushes → Eagle → Snake

8. In the food chain given below, X will be

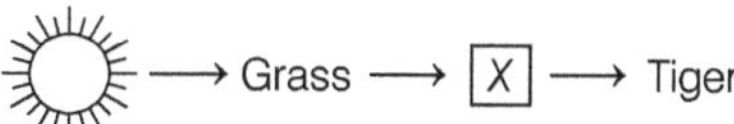

   (a) pond   (b) cockroach
   (c) deer   (d) sparrow

2 Marks Questions

9. Humans effect the environment in following ways

   I. Reforestation.

  II. Falling of tropical rainforests.

 III. Burning of fossil fuels.

 IV. Destroying habitats of animals for cultivation.

  V. Mining.

Which of these activities will lead to an increase in the level of CO_2 in the Earth's atmosphere?

Codes

(a) I, II and III   (b) II and III

(c) I, IV and V   (d) II, IV and V

10. Read the following statements.

Statement I Forests influence the climate and water cycle of a region.

Statement II Minimum land area cover for forests is 33%.

Which of the following statement is correct?

(a) Both I and II   (b) Only II

(c) Only I   (d) None of these

11. Refer to the food chain given below.

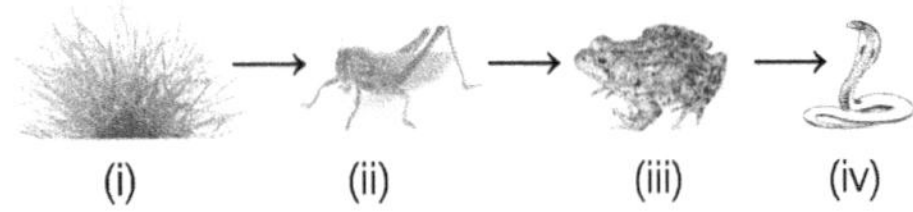

  (i)   (ii)   (iii)   (iv)

Identify the correct match for following statements

  I. The producer.

 II. Secondary consumer.

III. Herbivore.

Codes

      I   II   III   I   II   III

(a) (i) (iii) (ii)   (b) (iv) (ii) (i)

(c) (ii) (iv) (iii)   (d) (iii) (i) (iv)

12. Refer to the food web shown below.

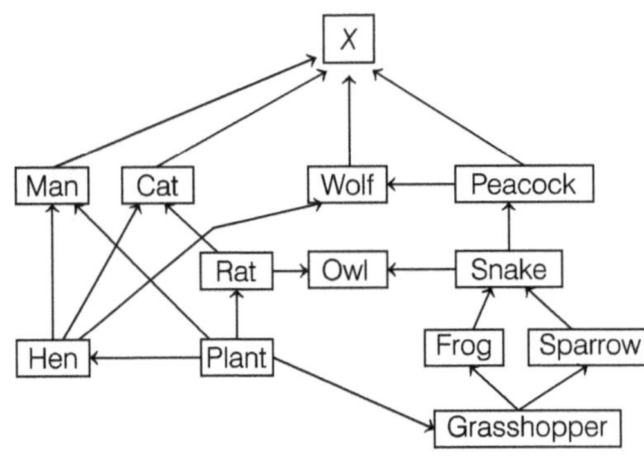

(a) X is most likely a decomposer organism.

(b) There are 5 secondary consumers in the given food web.

(c) There are 6 primary consumers in the food web.

(d) The inability of the oak to produce fruit would affect the snake more than the red tailed hawk.

13. Refer to the figure given below.

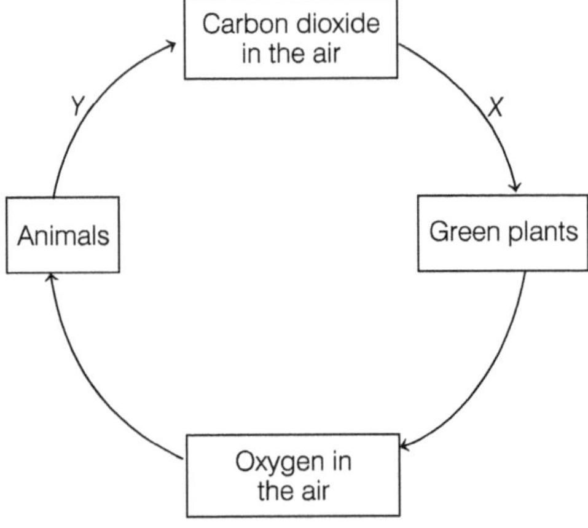

Which of the following statement is true for parts labelled X and Y?

  I. Plants and animals maintain the balance of oxygen and CO_2 in the air.

II. X could be transpiration through which excess water and O_2 is released *via* stomata.

III. Y could be decomposition which releases nutrients and gases trapped within the remains of dead organisms.

IV. X could be photosynthesis which absorbs CO_2 and releases O_2 in atmosphere.

V. Y could be respiration through which animals release CO_2 in the atmopshere.

Codes
(a) II and III
(b) I, IV and V
(c) I, II and IV
(d) I, III and V

14. Consider the following statements.

I. In absence of trees, soil will not hold water causing increased floods.

II. Autotrophs lie at the base of a food chain.

III. Branched part of a tree above the stem is called canopy.

IV. Secondary consumers enable the nutrients present in dead bodies of plant and animals to return to soil.

Select the option which correct identifies all the statements as true (T) or false (F).

Codes

	I	II	III	IV
(a)	F	F	T	T
(b)	T	F	F	F
(c)	T	T	F	F
(d)	F	T	T	T

PRACTICE SET 01

1 Mark Questions

1. Two bicycles are approaching each other with speed of 15 km/h. Initially, the distance between them is 60 km. How long will they hit each other?

  (a) 1 h   (b) 2 h
  (c) 3 h   (d) 4 h

2. Seema took some turmeric powder in a cup and made a paste by adding some water to it. Then, she take some paper strips and apply the paste over them. She dried the strips and use them to test the nature of following solution by keeping a few drops of the solution on the strips as shown below.

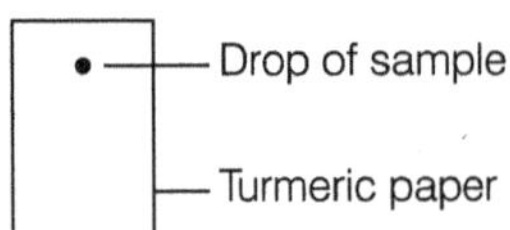

If the solutions used by her are
(i) solution of common salt
(ii) solution of baking soda
(iii) lemon juice (diluted) and
(iv) lime water, then the change in colour observed by her is

	(i)	(ii)	(iii)	(iv)
(a)	Yellow	Red	Yellow	Red
(b)	Yellow	Red	Red	Yellow
(c)	Yellow	Yellow	Red	Red
(d)	Red	Red	Yellow	Yellow

3. Observe the figure given below of excretory system and identify the part through which the waste carrying blood reach kidney and clean blood flows out of it.

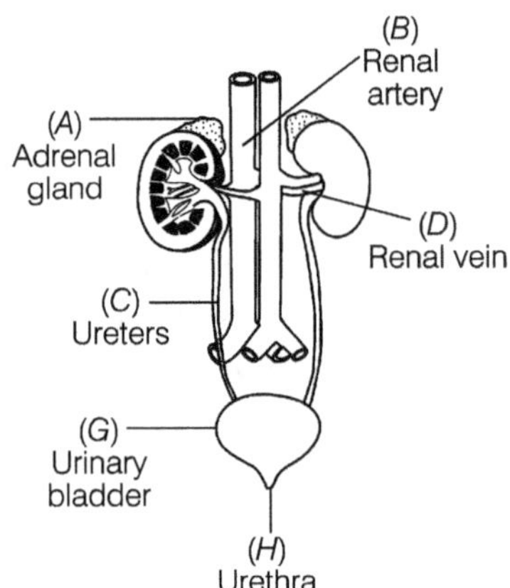

Choose the correct option.

	Waste blood carrier	Clean blood carrier
(a)	A	B
(b)	B	C
(c)	B	D
(d)	B	C

4. A mirror is tilted at an angle of 30° to a bench. A ray of light is directed, so that it hits the mirror at an angle of 20° to the surface of the mirror.

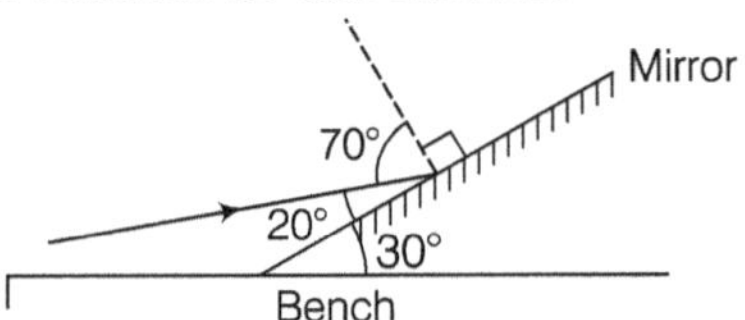

What is the angle of reflection?
  (a) 20°   (b) 50°
  (c) 30°   (d) 70°

5. Classify the following processes into physical changes *P* or chemical changes *C*.

  (i) Beating of aluminium metal to make aluminium foil.

 (ii) Digestion of food.

(iii) Cutting of a log of wood into pieces.

(iv) Burning of crackers.

  Codes

	(i)	(ii)	(iii)	(iv)
(a)	P	C	P	C
(b)	P	P	C	C
(c)	P	C	C	P
(d)	C	P	P	C

6. Consider the following statements.

  I. Wasp sting venom can be neutralised by an acid.

 II. Litmus indicators become green in neutral solution.

III. Salts obtained from nitric acid are called nitrates.

The correct statements are

  (a) I and II

  (b) II and III

  (c) I and III

  (d) I, II and III

Direction (Q. Nos. 7-9) Ah May leaves home at 8:15 am. She drives at 70 km/h to work. She reaches her office at 8:30 am.

7. How far is Ah May's office from her home?

  (a) 4.7 km

  (b) 17.5 km

  (c) 280 km

  (d) 1050 km

8. How fast must Ah May drive if she wants to reach her office at 8:25 am?

  (a) 47 km/h

  (b) 105 km/h

  (c) 170.5 km/h

  (d) 176.7 km/h

9. Ah May wants to reach her office by 8:15 am. but, because of the heavy traffic she can only travel at 50 km/h. What time would you advise Ah May to leave her home?

  (a) 7:30 am   (b) 7:40 am

  (c) 7:54 am   (d) 7:56 am

10. In which of the following circuits would the bulb light up?

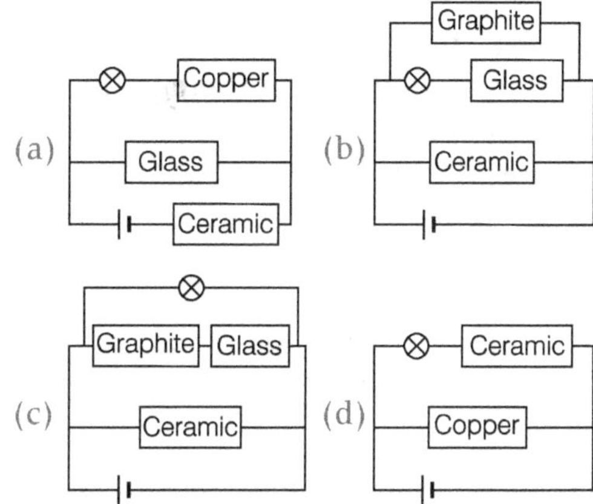

11. A convex lens is also called converging lens. Which statement about the image formed by a converging lens is correct?

  (a) It is always real and erect.

  (b) It is always real and inverted.

  (c) It is always virtual and erect.

  (d) It may be either real or erect.

12.

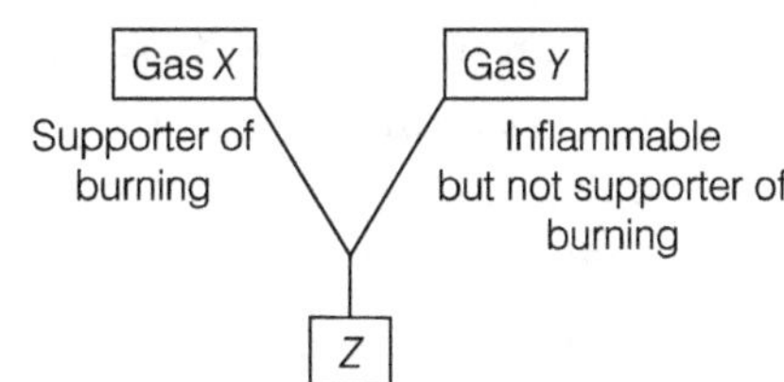

Liquid at room temperature
Used as extinguisher

The above process is an example of

  (a) reversible change

  (b) temporary change

  (c) physical change

  (d) chemical change

13. The diagram below shows three connecting wires from part of a circuit. The current in wire *RS* is 5 A and the current in wire *QR* is 2 A.

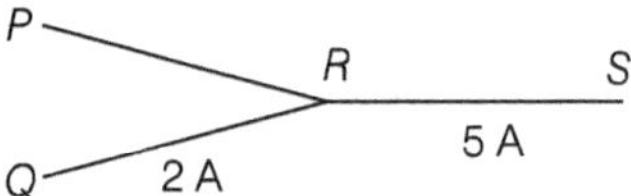

What will the current in wire *P R* be?
(a) 3 A   (b) 5 A   (c) 7 A   (d) 9 A

14. The diagrams below show two beakers *X* and *Y*, filled with different amounts of water. The water in both beakers is heated up to 80°C.

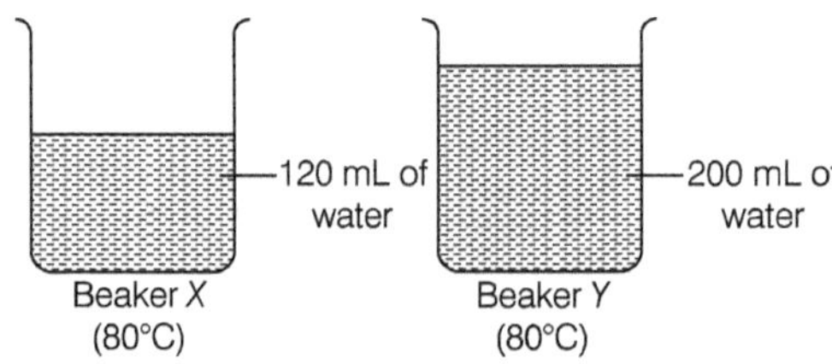

Which of the following statement is true about the two beakers of water?
(a) The water in both beakers has the same amount of heat energy and temperature.
(b) The water in both beakers has different amount of heat energy.
(c) The water in both beakers has the same amount of heat, but different amount of energy.
(d) The water in beaker *Y* will evaporate faster than the water in beaker *X*.

15. Some process along with their reversibility and chemical composition are tabulated below.

Process	Reversible	Chemical composition
I. Combustion	✗	Different
II. Crystallisation	✓	Different
III. Curd formation	✗	Same
IV. Digestion	✗	Same

Key ✓ Yes
     ✗ No

The correct matching(s) is/are
(a) I and II   (b) Only I
(c) I, III and IV   (d) All of these

16. Consider the given statements.
   I. In plants, the extra food is stored as starch.
   II. Minerals from soil travel throughout the plants through vascular tissues.
   III. Cortex lies in between the epidermis and vascular cylinder.
   IV. Sunlight and carbon dioxide enters into the leaves through stomata.
   V. *Cuscuta* is an example of a saprophytic plant.

Which of the above statement(s) is/are correct?
(a) I, II and III
(b) I and III
(c) Only III
(d) I and IV

Direction (Q. Nos. 17-19) The graph below shows the change in pH value of liquid *X* as liquid *Y* is mixed with it. One of the liquid is an acid and the other an alkali.

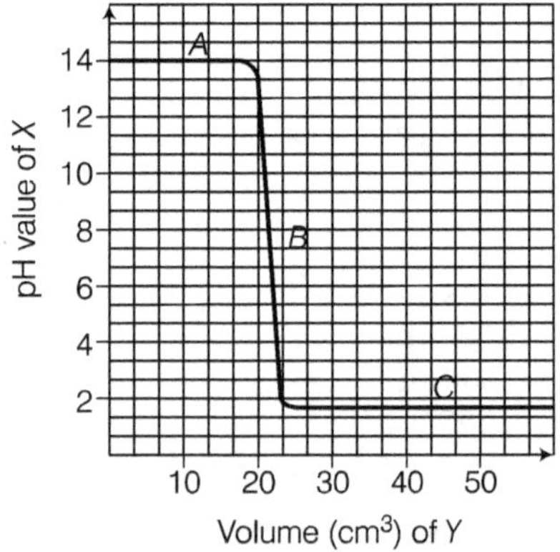

17. At which part of the curve will the red litmus paper turn blue?
(a) *A*   (b) *B*
(c) *C*   (d) *A, B* and *C*

18. What is the minimum volume of Y required to neutralise the solution?
(a) 10 mL
(b) 20 mL
(c) 30 mL
(d) 40 mL

19. What does part C of the graph indicate?
(a) X is in excess
(b) Y is in excess
(c) Y neutralises X completely
(d) Y neutralises X partially

20. Statement I For respiration, plants take in oxygen and release carbon dioxide.

Statement II Respiration is a chemical process which takes place with the release of heat energy.

Which of the above statement(s) is/are true?
(a) Only I
(b) Only II
(c) Both I and II
(d) Neither I nor II

21. Observe the table given below and identify P and Q.

Types of teeth	Permanent teeth	Milk teeth
M	4	4
N	8	8
Q	8	0
P	12	8
Total	**32**	**20**

Codes

	P	Q
(a)	Molars	Premolars
(b)	Canines	Incisors
(c)	Molars	Canines
(d)	Incisors	Premolars

22. Denise has a faulty digital thermometer. When she placed the thermometer in a bucket of ice, the reading obtained was 2°C.

When she placed it in a pot of boiling water, the new reading was 102°C. If the temperature reading of a glass of water at room temperature is 30°C, what is the actual temperature of the water?
(a) 34°C
(b) 32°C
(c) 28°C
(d) 26°C

23. The diagram shows a root hair, surrounded by a dilute solution of mineral ions.

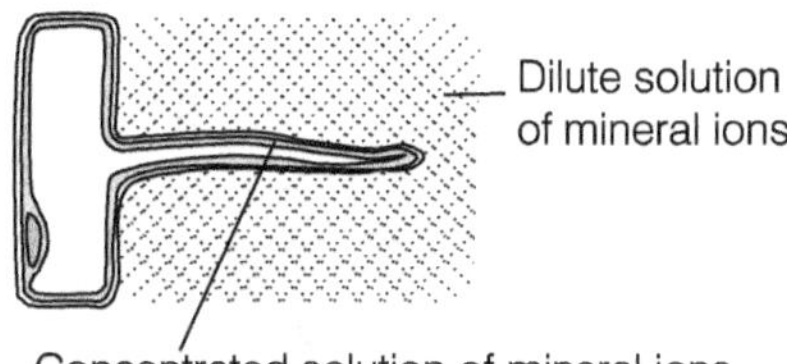

Which statement is correct?
(a) Water molecules move into the root hair by osmosis.
(b) Water molecules move out of the root hair by osmosis.
(c) Water molecules move into the root hair by diffusion.
(d) Water molecules move out of the root hair by diffusion.

24. Equal volumes of dilute hydrochloric acid and dilute sodium hydroxide are mixed. Which of the following represents the incorrect observation?
(a) Arrangement of atoms remains the same
(b) A neutral solution is formed
(c) Two new products are formed
(d) Heat is evolved

25. How do cyclones decreases the fertility of the soil in the coastal areas?
(a) By decreasing the water table of the place
(b) By dissolving soil and rocks
(c) By flooding the land with saline water
(d) By increasing the water table of the place

26. A substance having a temperature of 60°C is immersed in water which is at a temperature of 30°C. The temperature of the system will be
(a) 30°C
(b) 60°C
(c) More than 60°C
(d) In between 30°C and 60°C

27. Hot air balloons go up because
(a) hot air inside it is lighter than the surrounding air
(b) hot air inside it heavier than surrounding air
(c) air exerts pressure on the walls of the balloon
(d) Both (a) and (c)

28. Which is the best equation to represent aerobic respiration?
(a) Carbon dioxide + water + energy → oxygen + sugar
(b) Energy + oxygen → carbon dioxide + water + sugar
(c) Oxygen + sugar → carbon dioxide + water + energy
(d) Sugar + carbon dioxide → oxygen + water + energy.

29. In which of the following soil has highest water holding capacity?
(a) Sand soil
(b) Clayey soil
(c) Loamy soil
(d) Mixture of sand and loamy

30. Two pendulums *A* and *B* of masses 40g and 80g having same length is set into oscillation. The time period of oscillation is
(a) Greater for *A*
(b) Greater for *B*
(c) Same
(d) None of the above

31. In an electric bell, when the key is pushed, then
(a) The coil inside it behave like an electromagnet.
(b) The armature is attracted towards the coil.
(c) The clapper strikes the gong and produced sound.
(d) All of the above

32. Observe the given experimental set up

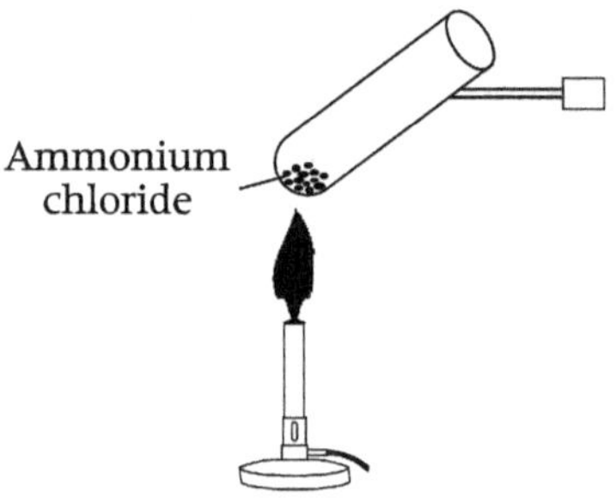

Which of the following represents the correct observation?
(a) Vapours of chlorine are evolved
(b) Ammonium chloride melts after some time
(c) White solid gets deposited on the upper cooler part of test tube
(d) Violet coloured vapours are produced as ammonium chloride undergoes sublimation

33. Look at the distance-time graphs of two moving vehicles and select the correct statement.

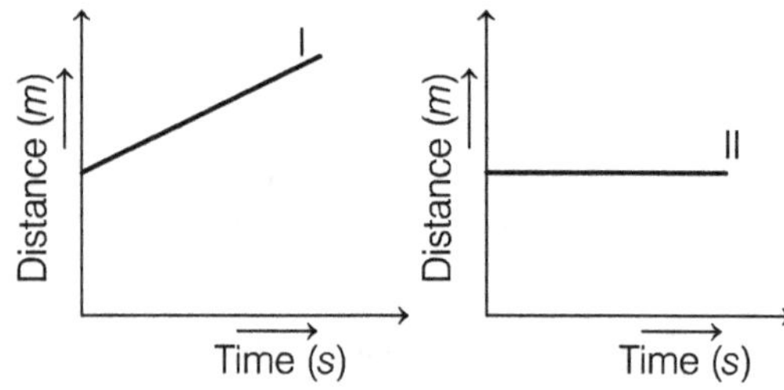

(a) Both the vehicles are moving with same constant speed.
(b) (I) is moving with constant speed and (II) is moving non-uniformly.
(c) (II) is moving with constant speed and (I) is moving non-uniformly.
(d) (I) is moving with constant speed but (II) is not in motion.

34. The diagram shows the structure of a flower. Where do pollination and fertilisation take place?

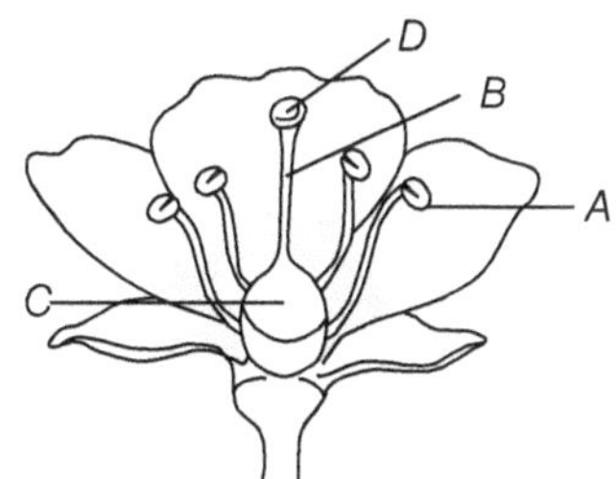

	Pollination	Fertilisation
(a)	C	D
(b)	D	C
(c)	A	B
(d)	D	B

35. During the beating of the heart, in which region will the highest pressure develop?
(a) Left atrium   (b) Left ventricle
(c) Pulmonary artery (d) Right ventricle

36. Vaishali is grouping fibres. She decides to draw a circle, a triangle and a rectangle to denote a particular type of fibre as shown below.

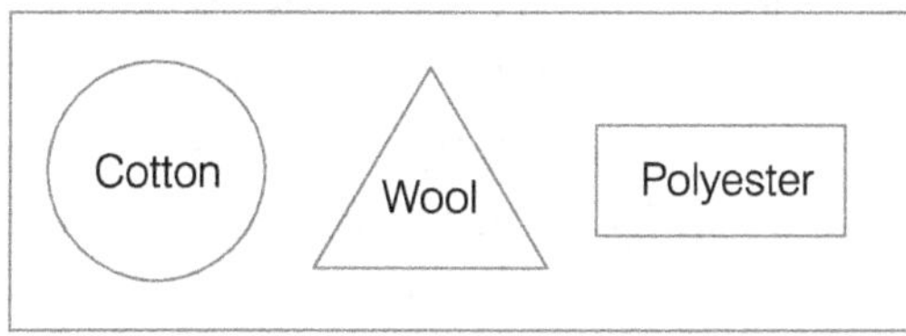

Which of the following sets of fibres could be correctly placed in each of the given boxes, respectively?

(a) Flax, silk, rayon
(b) Nylon, silk, flax
(c) Silk, rayon, nylon
(d) Silk, flax, rayon

37. When an object is placed at the centre of curvature of a concave mirror. Then, the image is formed
(a) between focus and centre of curvature
(b) at the centre of curvature
(c) at the principal focus
(d) beyond centre of curvature

38. The cells shown in figure can be found in the blood.

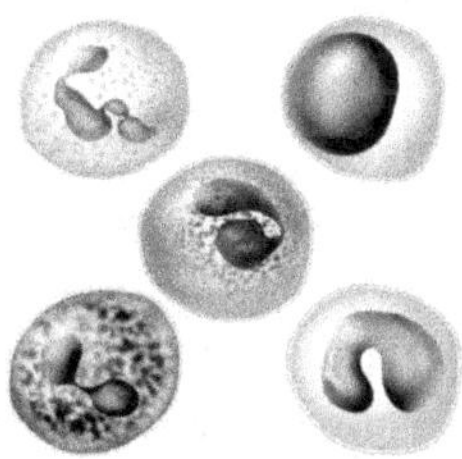

Which of the following statement(s) is/are correct regarding these cells?
(a) They do not have nucleus.
(b) They help the body to fight against infections.
(c) They help the blood to clot.
(d) They help to transport oxygen.

39. Which of the following statement is incorrect?
(a) In winter, the wind blows from the land towards the ocean
(b) In winter, the wind blows from the ocean towards the land
(c) In summer, the winds blows from the ocean towards the land
(d) Both (a) and (c)

40. Which of the following represents a displacement reaction?
(a) Iron nails kept in open
(b) Iron nails kept in copper sulphate solution
(c) Iron nails kept in water
(d) All of the above

2 Marks Questions

41. Which of the following correctly shows the direction of the convection currents when water is heated?

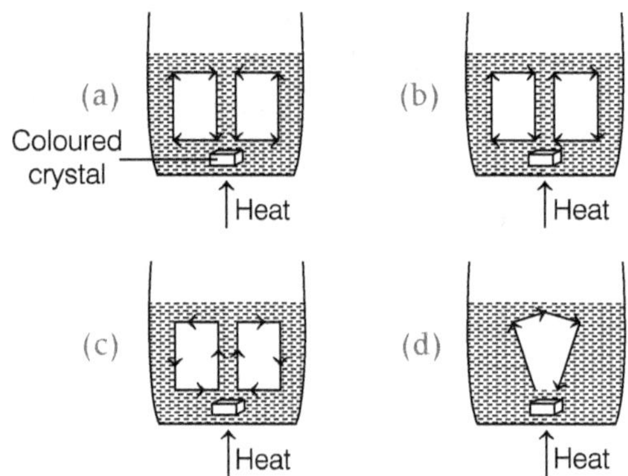

42. Which of the following statement is incorrect?

Statement I Asexual reproduction does not require two opposite sexes.

Statement II New organisms are formed by the fusion of ovum and sperm.

Statement III Reproduction in plants done by asexual reproduction.

Codes
(a) Statements I and III
(b) Statements III and II
(c) Statements II and I
(d) Statements I only

43. Study the given diagram and choose the correct option.

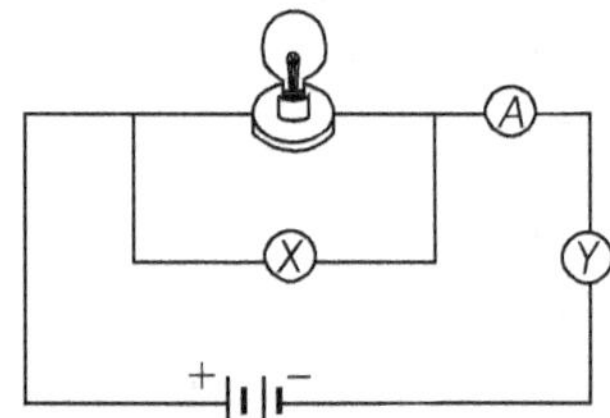

X is a component used to measure voltage across the bulb and Y is component used to control the circuit. X and Y are

	X	Y
(a)	Voltmeter	Ammeter
(b)	Ammeter	Voltmeter
(c)	Ammeter	Key
(d)	Voltmeter	Key

44. Tina ate Lemon and felt stomach burn. She had milk of magnesia ($(MG(OH)_2)$) to neutralize her stomach.

She wanted to test both substance on litmus raper what observation(s) is/are correct?

	Lemon	Milk of magnesia $(Mg(OH)_2)$
(a)	Turns blue litmus into red	Turns blue litmus into red
(b)	Turns red litmus into blur	Turns red litmus into blue
(c)	Turns blue litmus into red	Turns red litmus into blue
(d)	Turns red litmus into blue	Turns blue litmus into red

What colours will be obtained if each of the indicators are added separately to distilled water?

Codes

	P	Q	R	S
(a)	Colourless	Red	Red	Blue
(b)	Colourless	Yellow	Blue	Blue
(c)	Red	Yellow	Blue	Colourless
(d)	Colourless	Yellow	Red	Colourless

45. Read the given statements below and identify the incorrect statements.

Statement I Blood is of red colour due to the presence of RBC's which contain haemoglobin.

Statement II RBC's in blood fight against the foreign particles that can harm our body.

Codes
(a) Statement I
(b) Statement II
(c) Both statements are incorrect
(d) None of the above

46. In a vacuum flask, which method of heat transfer are prevented by the vacuum?
(a) Conduction only   (b) Convection only
(c) Radiation only   (d) Both (a) and (b)

47. Refer to the given description of parts of plants and identify A, B, C, D and E.

Description of parts of plants

A. Opening and closing of stomata.
B. Fluid matrix in a chloroplast.
C. Tiny vessels that transport water from roots of a plants to its leaves.
D. Vessels that transport food from leaves to the other parts of the plant.
E. Edges of leaves.

Codes

	A	B	C	D	E
(a)	Guard cells	Stroma	Xylem	Phloem	Lamina
(b)	Stroma	Cytoplasm	Phloem	Xylem	Lamina
(c)	Guard cells	Lamina	Stroma	Xylem	Phloem
(d)	Lamina	Cytoplasm	Xylem	Phloem	Stroma

48. State whether the following are true (T) or false (F).

I. The West coast of India is more vulnerable to cyclonic storms.
II. Do not take shelter in open garage, storage sheds in case a storm is accompanied by lightening.
III. The energy required to form and sustain a cyclone comes from the heat of condensation of water vapour.
IV. An East ward shift in the wind current is observed due to revolution of Earth.

Codes

	I	I	III	IV			I	I	III	IV
(a)	T	F	F	T	(b)	T	F	T	F
(c)	F	T	T	F	(d)	F	F	T	T

49. There is a flow chart given below, it shows the components involved in the replenishment of nutrients in soil. Identify P, Q, R and S.

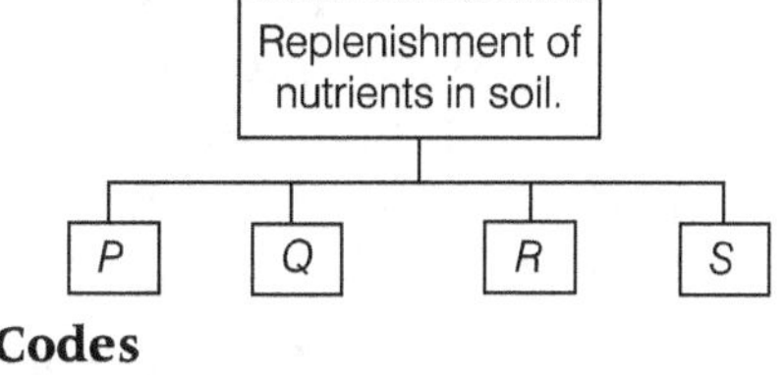

Codes

	P	Q	R	S
(a)	Cattle dung	Saprophytes	Compost	Fertilisers
(b)	Parasitic plants	Carbon dioxide	Fertilisers	Cattle dung
(c)	Fertilisers	Cattle dung	Compost	Leguminous crops
(d)	Chlorophyll	Carbon dioxide	Compost	Fertilisers

50. Given below is a section of leaf in which A, B and C are marked.

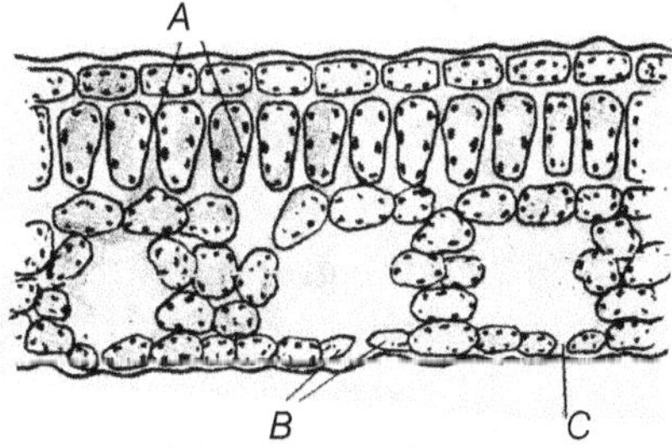

Identify the correct statement regarding A, B and C.

Statement I 'A' helps in capturing energy for the process of photosynthesis.

Statement II 'B' helps in opening and closing of 'C'.

Codes
(a) Statement I is correct
(b) Statement II is correct
(c) Both statements are correct
(d) None of the above

PRACTICE SET 02

1 Mark Questions

1. A helicopter takes 5 min to travel from terminal X to terminal Y. If the distance between terminals X and Y is 2000 m, then which of the following is the average speed of the helicopter?
(a) 24 km/h   (b) 40 km/h
(c) 400 km/h   (d) 440 km/h

2. The diagram shows a section of a stem. Which tissue transports sugars and amino acids from the leaves to other parts of the plant?

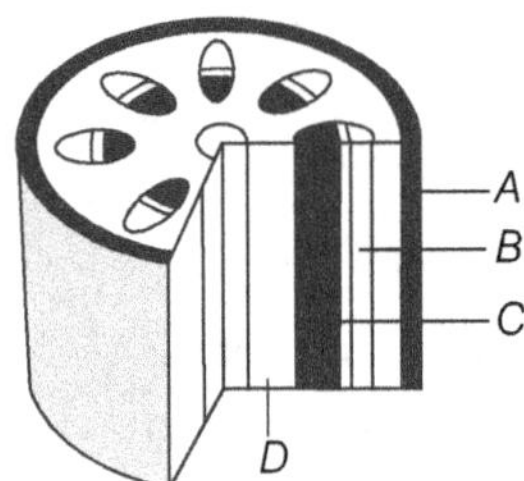

Codes
(a) B (b) A
(c) D (d) C

3. The distance-time graph of an object in motion is shown as below

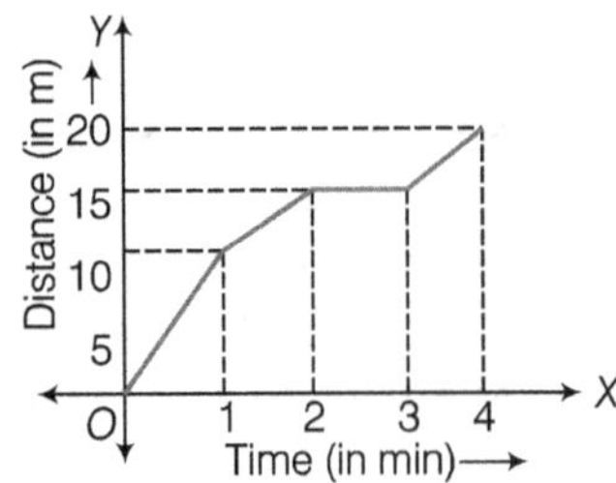

What will be the average speed of the object?
(a) 1 ms^{-1} (b) 2 ms^{-1}
(c) 0.5 ms^{-1} (d) 0.08 ms^{-1}

4. Match the items of Column I with Column II.

Column I	Column II
A. Large crystals	1. Turns lime water milky
B. Depositing a layer of zinc on iron	2. Physical change
C. Souring of milk	3. Rust
D. Carbon dioxide	4. Sugar candy (mishri)
E. Iron oxide	5. Chemical change
F. Dissolving common salt in water	6. Galvanisation

Codes

	A	B	C	D	E	F
(a)	4	6	1	5	3	1
(b)	4	4	1	3	5	2
(c)	4	6	5	1	3	2
(d)	4	5	6	1	2	3

5. An object is placed in front of a spherical mirror. The image formed by the spherical mirror is virtual. The mirror will be
(a) concave
(b) convex
(c) Either (a) or (b)
(d) metallic

6. If one litre of water at 20°C is mixed with one litre of water at 60°C. The temperature of mixture will be
(a) 80°C
(b) 10°C
(c) between 20°C and 60°C
(d) 60°C

7. Which device is used in Jantar Mantar to measure time?
(a) Sand dial   (b) Sun dial
(c) Sand clock   (d) Quartz dial

8. The main principle used in ancient time to measure time is
(a) position of Moon in the sky
(b) position of Sun in the sky
(c) Both (a) and (b)
(d) Neither (a) nor (b)

9. A car takes 10 h to travel from town *A* to town *B* and 7 h to travel from town *B* to town *C*.

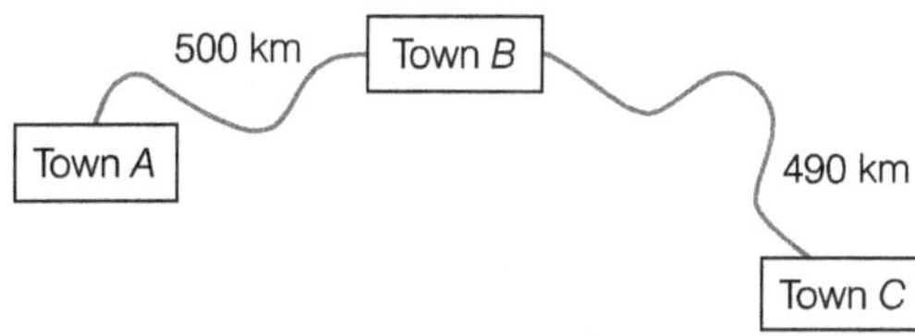

What is the average speed of the car in the whole journey?
(a) 116.47 km/h
(b) 29.12 km/h
(c) 58.24 km/h
(d) 60 km/h

10. Modern clocks are based on
(a) number of heart beats
(b) number of vibrations of quartz crystal
(c) number of ticks of second hand in a clock
(d) None of the above

11. Which of the following is the correct diagram when light passes through a piece of glass?

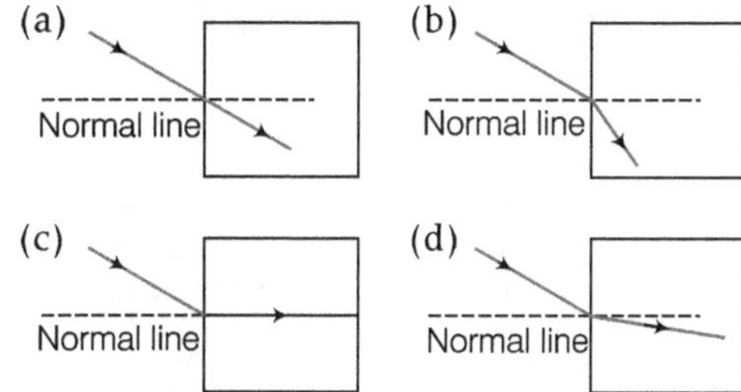

12. The diagrams below show the passage of light through glass blocks. Which diagram is not correct?

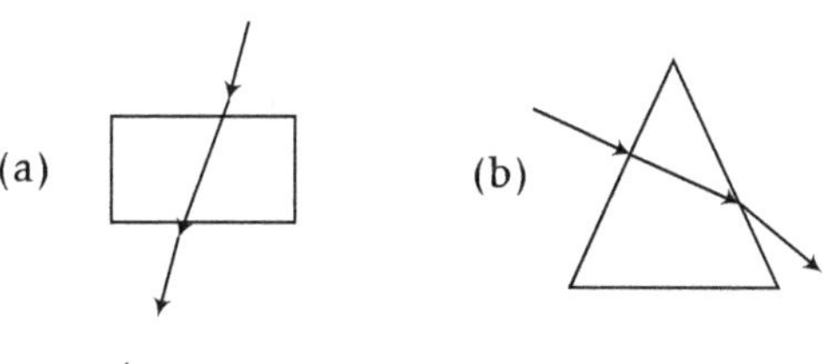
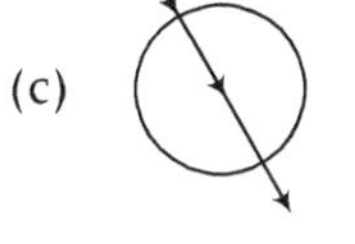
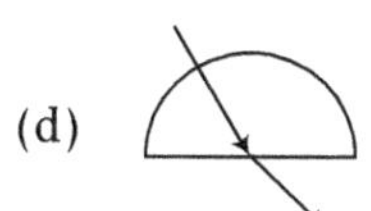

13.

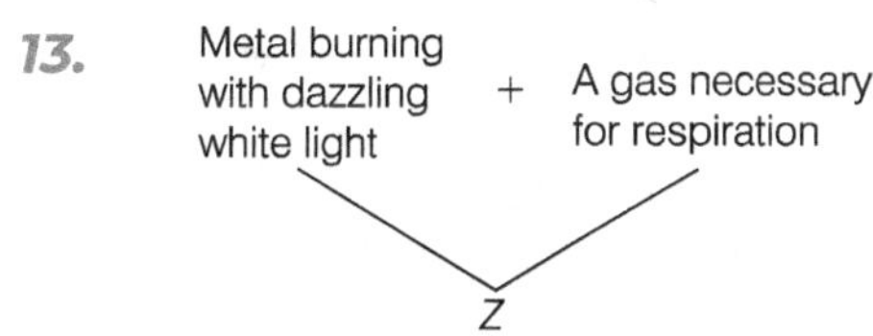

Z is
(a) magnesium oxide
(b) manganese dioxide
(c) magnesium carbonate
(d) magnesium sulphate

14. Which of the following statements about alkalis is not true?
(a) Alkalis taste bitter and feel slippery.
(b) Alkalis can be corrosive and hence need to be handled carefully.
(c) Alkalis turn phenolphthalein colourless.
(d) Alkalis turn red litmus paper blue.

15. The figure below shows a mercury thermometer. The distance between $-10°C$ and $110°C$ is 30 cm.

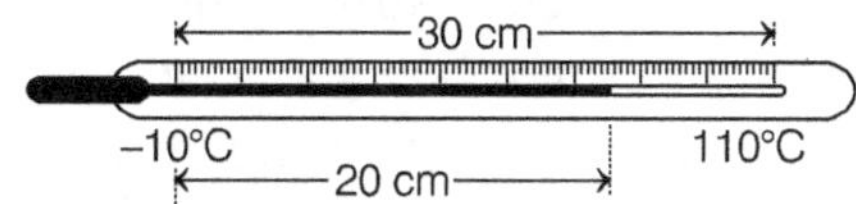

At what temperature will the mercury thread be 20 cm long?
(a) 67°C   (b) 70°C
(c) 73°C   (d) 80°C

16. Which of the following circuits produce the brightest bulbs?

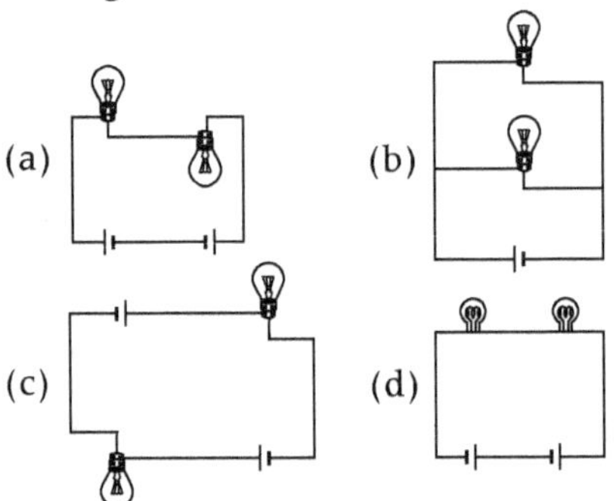

17. Factories are allowed to flow their wastes into river water only after its proper treatment. Which of the following shows the correct treatment and reason for applying this?
(a) Sorting, as bigger wastes pollutes river the most
(b) Detoxification, as the wastes may contain poisonous substances.
(c) Neutralisation, as the waste is acidic and will kill the aquatic life.
(d) Decomposition as the waste may contain several chemicals

18.

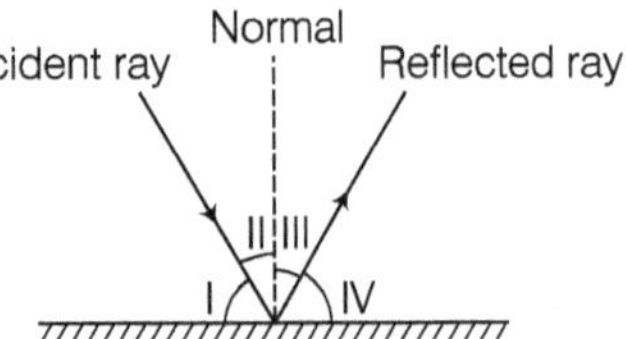

Which of the angles shown above is the angle of reflection?
(a) I　　(b) II　　(c) III　　(d) IV

19. Due to overloading and short-circuit, electrical circuits suffer a huge damage. Which of the following devices is used to prevent the flow of excess current in a circuit?
(a) Switch　(b) Bulb　(c) Fuse　　(d) Wire

20. During rainy season, you can see a number of earthworms around you. They look little moist. This is because of ....*A*.... . The respiration is called ...*B*... .

	A	B
(a)	Water transport in their body	Pulmonary respiration
(b)	Rainy season	Branchial respiration
(c)	Their living habitat is under the soil	Tracheal respiration
(d)	They exchange respiratory gases through skin	Cutaneous respiration

21. The heating of seawater is called ...... and the product(s) is/are ....
(a) boiling, hydrogen and oxygen
(b) evaporation, salt and steam
(c) electrolysis, salt and water
(d) crystallisation, salt and water

22. Which of the following would happen when an acid is slowly added to an alkaline solution?
　I. The acid would lose its properties.
　II. The alkali would lose its properties.
III. The pH value of the acid will increase.
IV. The pH value of the alkaline solution will decrease.

Codes
(a) I and III　　　　(b) II and IV
(c) I, II and IV　　　(d) All of these

23. Mannu was investigating how a certain factor affected the growth of plants. The table shows how the experiment was set up.

	Location of pot	Soil	Water	Number of seeds in each pot	Number of earthworms in the soil
Pot A	Window ledge	Garden Soil	500 mL	2	8
Pot B	Window ledge	Garden Soil	500 mL	10	8

Which of the following characteristics of the seedlings should Mannu observe to tell which pot of plant was growing better?
(a) Colour of the leaves
(b) Height of the seedlings
(c) Thickness of the seedlings
(d) Both (a) and (b)

24. When electric current is passed through an electromagnet, it behaves like a temporary magnet. Which of the following figures correctly depicts the direction of magnetic field lines?

(a) 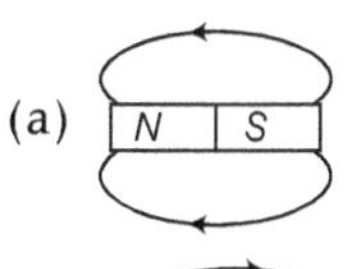
(b) 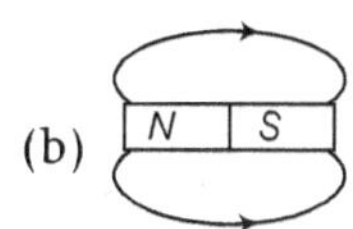
(c) 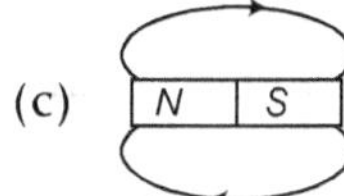
(d) 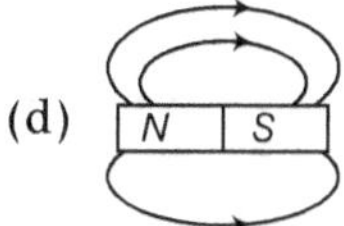

25. Rama went to a shop to buy some cooking utensils. She asked the shopkeeper, why the cooking utensils are always fitted with plastic handles?
(a) Plastics are good thermal conductor.
(b) Plastics are not strong.
(c) Plastics are poor thermal conductor.
(d) Plastics have a high density.

26. The diagram below shows some of the food molecules which are digested to become small molecules by the action of enzymes.

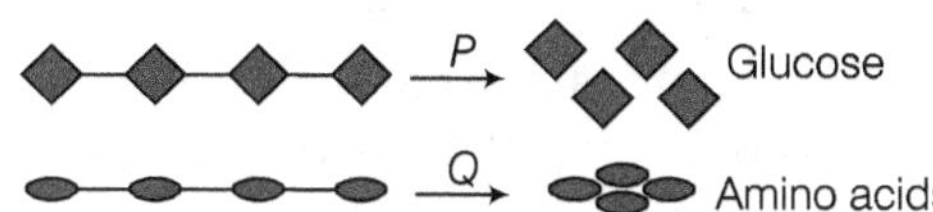

What are the enzymes P and Q?

	P	Q
(a)	Carbohydrase	Protease
(b)	Lipase	Carbohydrase
(c)	Protease	Lipase
(d)	Amylase	Carbohydrase

27. In which of the following parts of the digestive system is hydrochloric acid produced?

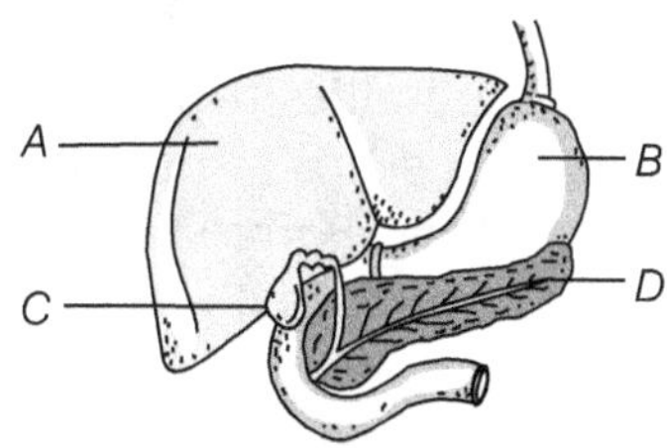

(a) A (b) B
(c) C (d) D

28. One of the ways to prevent us from getting electric shock is by wearing rubber shoes. What is the reason?
(a) Rubber is a very good insulator.
(b) Shoes are placed at the lowest part of our body.
(c) All metals conduct electricity except shoes.
(d) Copper conducts electricity better than rubber.

29. When you stand on bare feet with one foot on a stone floor and the other on a carpet, the stone floor feels colder than the carpet. What is the most likely explanation?
(a) Air is unable to circulate through the carpet fibres.
(b) The stone is at a lower temperature than the carpet.
(c) More heat energy flows from the carpet to your foot than from the stone floor to your foot.
(d) More heat energy flows from your foot to the stone floor than from your foot to the carpet.

30. Consider the following statements.
   I. It is made up of living cells.
   II. It helps in the transport of food and hormones in the plants.
   III. Structurally, its cells join end to end.
   IV. Its cells form sieve plates.

Which of the following structural component is this?
(a) Cambium   (b) Tracheids
(c) Xylem   (d) Phloem

31. This is a bimetallics trip. It is made up of 2 different strips of metals, X and Y joined together. Before heating, the strips are of the same length.

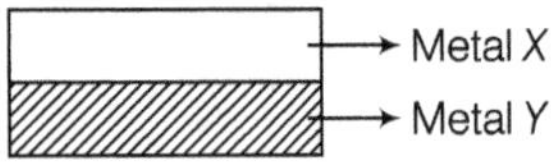

After heating, the following is observed.

The following inference can be deduced from the above observation.
(a) Metal X is better conductor of heat.
(b) Metal Y is better conductor of heat.
(c) Metal X is poor insulator.
(d) Metal Y is poor insulator.

32. Consider the following statements.
  I. The common name of hydrochloric acid is aqua fortis.
  II. Acids taste sour.
  III. Term alkali is used for water soluble bases.
The incorrect statement(s) is/are
(a) I and II   (b) II and III
(c) Only I   (d) Only III

33. Which of the following are similarities between acids and alkalis?
  I. Both are colourless liquids.
  II. Both are hazardous when concentrated.
  III. Their pH value decreases to 7 when they are neutralised.
  IV. Both contain water.

  Codes
  (a) I and II   (b) III and IV
  (c) I, II and IV   (d) All of these

34. After studying photosynthesis, Neelima drew the illustration of a plant shown below.

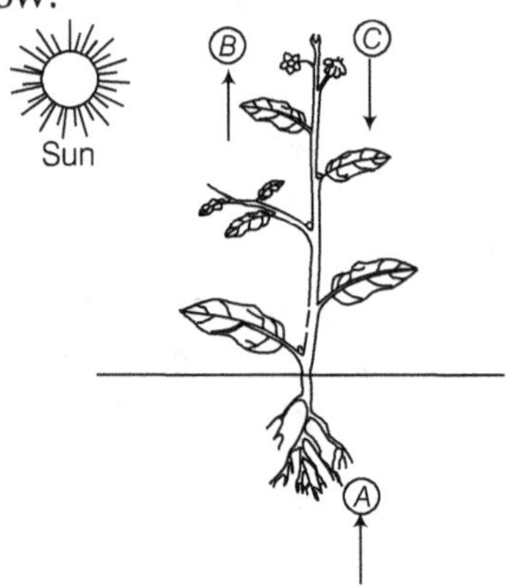

Arrow A represents
(a) release of water and minerals by the plant into soil
(b) release of carbon dioxide into the soil
(c) absorption of water and minerals by the roots from the soil
(d) release of oxygen into the atmosphere

35. Consider the following figure shown below. Which of the following processes are involved in the figure?

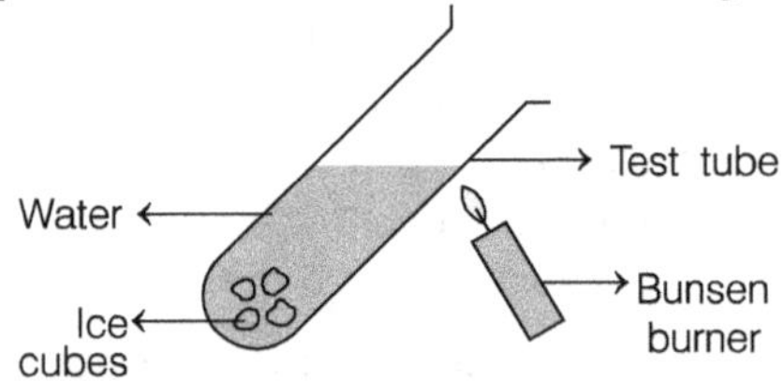

(a) Conduction and melting.
(b) Insulation and heating.
(c) Conduction and contraction.
(d) Expansion and contraction.

36. Mr. Sharma started a shipping corporation but he was facing huge loss because of the rusting of iron ships. What was the cause and solution to this problem?
(a) The bodies of the ships are in contact of salty water, so he can paint the ships
(b) The bodies of the ships are in contact of salty seawater, so galvanisation is a solution to it

(c) The bodies of the ships are not made up of good quality metal, so he must improve the quality of metal

(d) The bodies of the ships are in contact of non-salty water, so he can paint them

37. Study the three glasses of tea that are placed on the table.

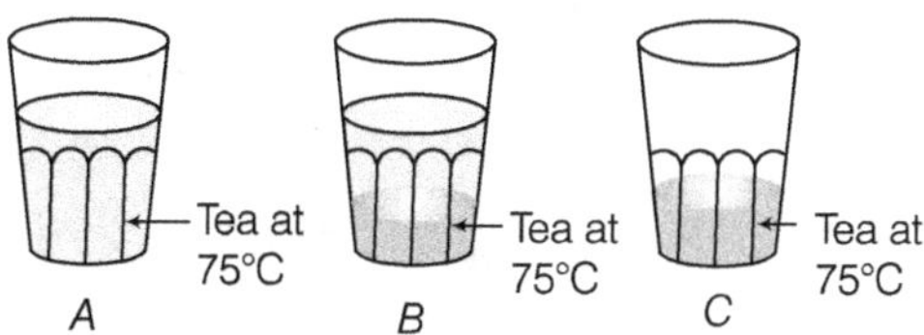

Which of the following statements are true about the glasses of tea?

I. The tea in the three glasses have the same amount of heat.

II. The tea in the three glasses are at the same temperature.

III. There is more heat in glass A than in glass B.

IV. There is less heat in glass C than in glass B.

V. More heat is needed to warm up glass B than glass C.

Codes
(a) I and II   (b) II and III
(c) III and IV   (d) II, III and V

38. Eric conducted an experiment to find out which material was a better conductor of heat. He placed four identical spoons made up of silver, copper, aluminium and iron into a beaker of very hot water.

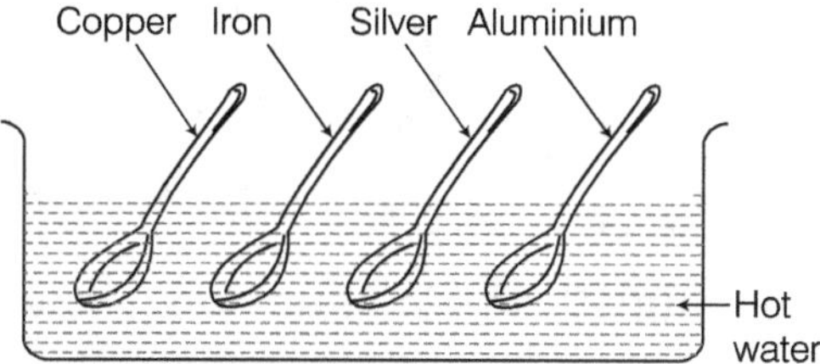

Rank the spoons from the best to the worst conductor of heat.
(a) copper, silver, iron, aluminium
(b) copper, iron, aluminium, silver
(c) silver, iron, copper, aluminium
(d) silver, copper, aluminium, iron

39. The ammeter reading in the following circuit diagrams consisting of a cell, a resistor, a key and an ammeter will be

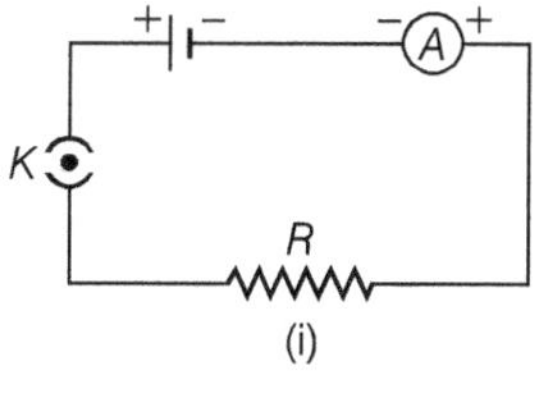

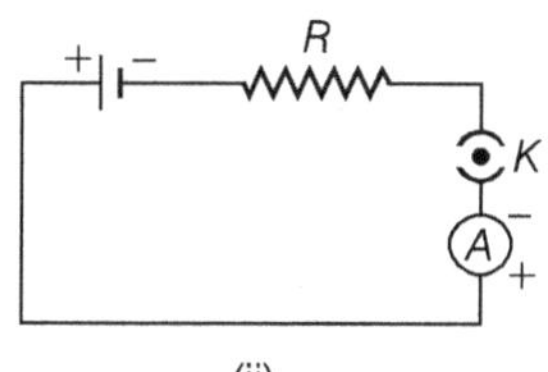

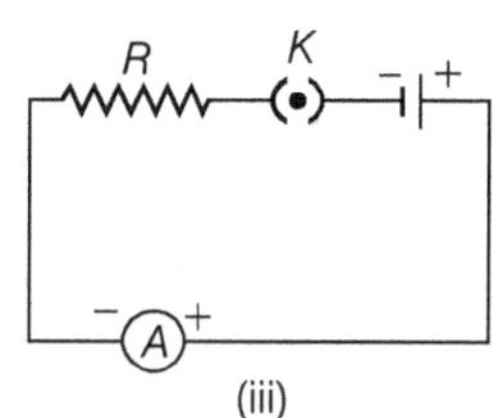

(a) Maximum in (i)
(b) Maximum in (ii)
(c) Maximum in (iii)
(d) Same in all the cases

40. Cooler air from 0 to 30 degree latitudes on either side of the equator moves towards the equator. These winds blow towards the equator are
(a) Trade winds
(b) Westerlies
(c) Easterlies
(d) Both (b) and (c)

2 Marks Questions

41. Refer to the diagrams below which show the transverse sections of a young root and three types of cell found in it.

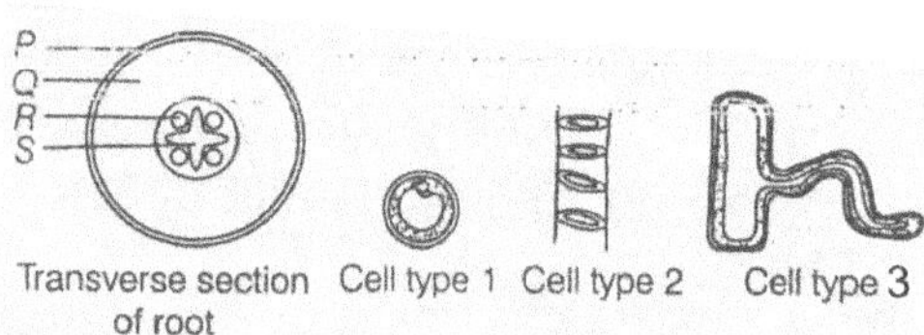

Which of the following correctly lists the locations of the three types of cells and correctly state the function of P, Q and R?

	Cell type 1, Function of P	Cell type 2, Function of Q	Cell type 3, Function of R
(a)	Q, Protection	P, Food storage	S, Transport
(b)	Q, Absorption	S, Protection	P, Food storage
(c)	R, Transport	Q, Food storage	P, Protection
(d)	R, Absorption	P, Support	S, Transport

42. The diagram shows a section through the heart.

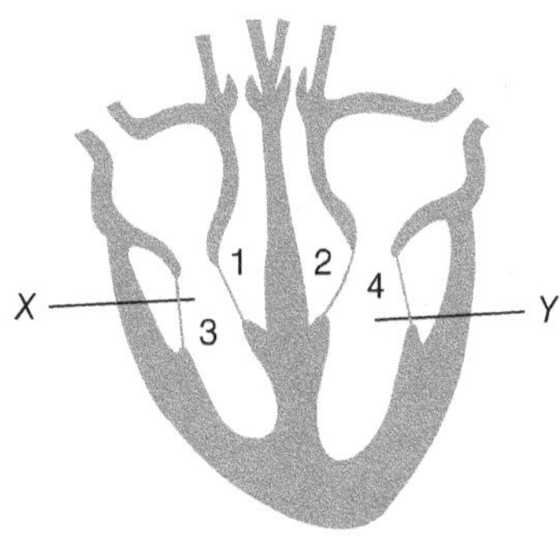

While chambers X and Y are emptying blood, which valves are open and which are closed?

	Valves 1 and 2	Valves 3 and 4
(a)	Closed	Closed
(b)	Open	Closed
(c)	Closed	Open
(d)	Open	Open

43.

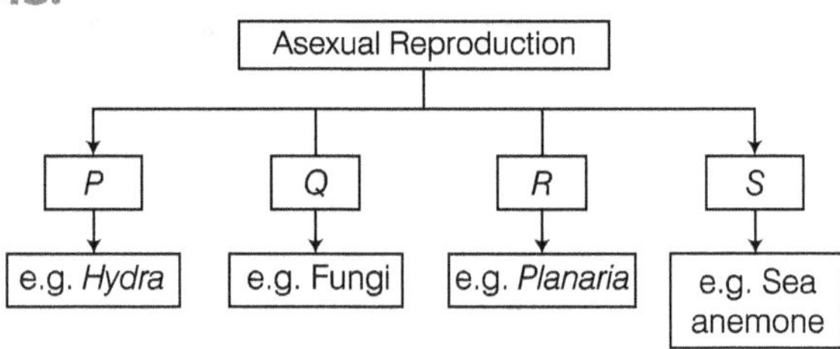

Use your analytical skills and observe the above flow chart. Identify P, Q, R and S correctly.

Codes

	P	Q	R	S
(a)	Binary fission	Budding	Regeneration	Fragmentation
(b)	Budding	Spore formation	Regeneration	Fragmentation
(c)	Spore formation	Budding	Fragmentation	Regeneration
(d)	Budding	Binary fission	Fragmentation	Regeneration

44. The chain of boxes given below show a type of process occurring in plants.

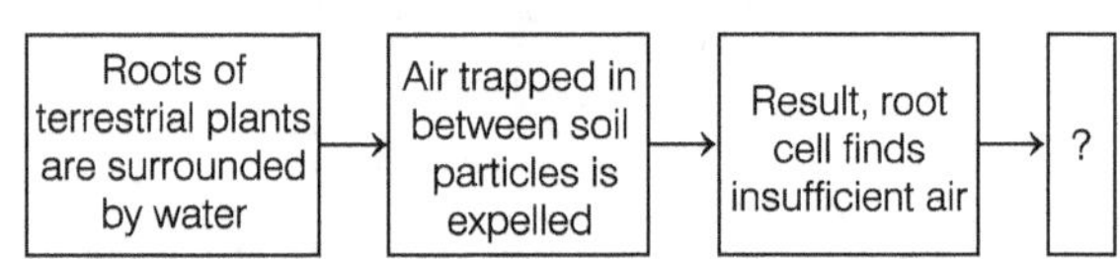

Identify the option from the following that correctly fills the last box.

Codes
(a) The plant will die
(b) The plant will start aerobic respiration
(c) The plant will start photosynthesis
(d) The plant will start anaerobic respiration

45. Consider the following circuits and choose the one in which all the components are connected properly.

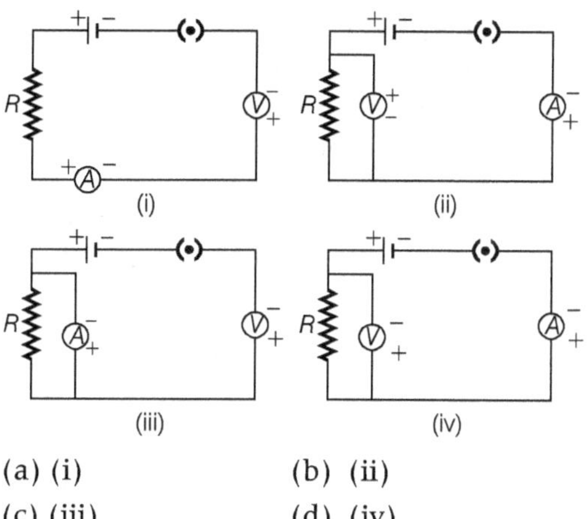

(a) (i)   (b) (ii)
(c) (iii)   (d) (iv)

46. Above plant mushroom gets its food from .... The type of nutrition is ....

Mushroom

A. From dead and decaying plants.
B. From photosynthesis.
C. By eating small insects which come near it.
D. From the water we pour near it.
1. Parasitic.
2. Autotrophic.
3. Saprophytic.
4. Symbiotic.

Codes
(a) A–3   (b) B–2
(c) C–1   (d) D–4

47.

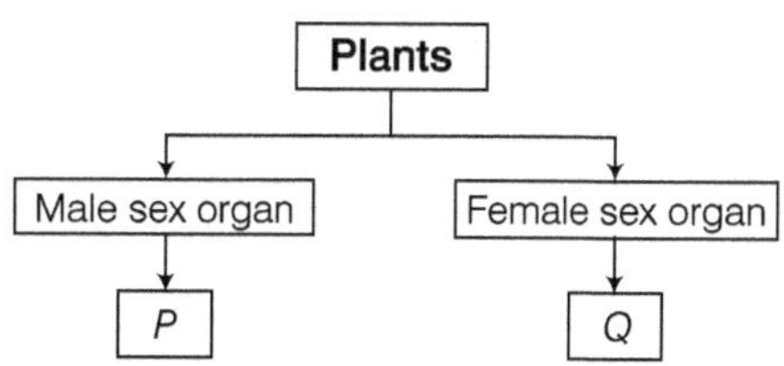

Observe the above flow chart carefully. Identify P and Q with their respective description.
(a) P–stamen, it contains pollen grains Q–carpel, its lower part is ovary that contains ovule.
(b) P–carpel, it contains pollen grains. Q–stamen, it contains ovule which is the lower part of ovary.
(c) P–pistil, it contains ovule. Q–style, it contains pollen grains.
(d) P–style, it contains pollen grains. Q–pistil, it is the lower part of the ovary that contains ovule.

48. Sarita while helping her mother in kitchen work noticed that the slice of potato and brinjal have acquired a brown colour. She asked her mother reason behind this change. Her mother said whenever we keep cut pieces of these vegetables open for a long time they acquire such colour.
I. Cutting vegetable is a physical change and change in colour is a chemical change.
II. Vegetable acquire brown colour due to chemical reaction.
III. Change in brown colour is a reversible process.
Codes
(a) I and II
(b) II only
(c) I, II and III
(d) II and III

49. Root hair absorb water

↓

Take it to xylem tube

↓

Xylem tubes reach to leaves of plant. Observe the above flow of steps that shows the job of root hair. Which of the following statement is correct regarding this?

  I. Water enters into xylem vessels through root hair, where vessels are formed by dead cells.

 II. Root hair lie in between soil particles.

III. The cells of xylem vessels have tapering ends.

IV. Cells of xylem vessels are joined with open ends.

Codes

(a) I and II

(b) II and III

(c) I, II and IV

(d) None of the above

50. On a cold day, it is hard to open the lid of a tight container. But when you gently heat the neck you can easily open the lid. Why?

(a) On heating glass expands and lid contracts

(b) Lid expends more than the neck and thus slides easily

(c) Neck becomes slippery on heating

(d) Lids of the bottles cannot bear the heat

Hints & Solutions

Nutrition in Plants

1. (a) P is water and Q is sugar, leaves take up water from the soil for the preparation of food by the process of photosynthesis. Food (sugar) from the leaves are transported to other parts of plants with the help of phloem.
Whereas water is transported to all parts of plants from roots through xylem.

2. (a) During photosynthesis, light energy splits water into oxygen and hydrogen ions. Carbon dioxide gas combines with the hydrogen to make glucose.
So, if oxygen (^{18}O) is incorporated into water, then radioactive ^{18}O will be found only in oxygen.

3. (c) The part labelled as 'X' is chloroplast. It is present in leaf that contains the pigment chlorophyll. This pigment traps light energy from the Sun for plants to conduct photosynthesis.

4. (c) In insectivorous plants, the nutrition is derived by trapping and digesting insects who sits on their leaves. For this action, the leaves of insectivorous plants are modified into pitchers to trap insects, e.g. *Nepenthes*.

5. (c) The analogy is completed as,
Cuscuta : Parasite : : *Rhizopus* : Saprophyte.
Parasites derive nutrition by living in or outside a host's body, while saprophytes derive nutrition from dead and decaying organic matter. *Cuscuta* is an example of a parasite, whereas *Rhizopus* is an example of a saprophyte.

6. (b) The relationship is symbiotic where both the organisms are deriving benefits from each other.

7. (b) Fungi are saprotrophs, i.e. they feed on dead and decaying organic matter. They secrete digestive juice and absorb nutrients released by them. This helps in fastening the process of natural decomposition. Hence, they are also called as decomposers.

8. (c) *Rhizobium* lives in symbiotic relationship within the roots of leguminous plants. It fixes atmospheric N_2 into a soluble form for plants and in return, it receives food and shelter from plants.

9. (c) The figure shows mushrooms (fungi). These are saprotrophs, i.e., they derive nutrients from dead and decaying organic matter, e.g. dead animals, wood, cow dung, etc.

10. (c) In group (c), algae and *Cactus* are autotrophic plants, while rabbit is a heterotrophs as it depends on plants for its nutrition.

11. (c) The gas X is nitrogen. Plants cannot able to use atmospheric nitrogen directly therefore it needs to be converted into another forms so as to get utilised by plants. *Rhizobium* bacteria play this role by converting atmospheric nitrogen into nitrate or ammonium forms.

12. (b) This experiment shows that oxygen is released during the process of photosynthesis. This is because O_2 is the component of air which supports burning.

13. (b) This experiment is used to demonstrate that carbon dioxide is essential for photosynthesis to occur.
CO_2 is taken in through the stomata of leaves.

14. (c) The iodine solution will turn bluish black due to the presence of starch in it.

15. (c) The correct sequence of this activity is as follows
   C. A green leaf is plucked from a plant.
   B. The leaf is boiled in alcohol in a water bath.
   D. Leaf is washed to remove any traces of chlorophyll.
   A. Iodine solution is poured on the leaf, which turns the leaf blue black colour.

16. (b) The part labelled A is the leaf of a pitcher plant. It traps insects for nutrition. This type of feeding method is known as insectivorous mode, a type of heterotrophic nutrition.

17. (b) The organisms is a fungus, i.e. *Rhizopus* which grows on moist surfaces. It has a saprotrophic mode of nutrition, i.e. it derives nutrition from dead or decaying substances.

18. (c) The set up (c) will have least amount of carbon dioxide. This is because the *Hydrilla* plant will use all the CO_2 for photosynthesis. Since no living organism is present in set up, only O_2 will be present here in set up (c).

19. (c) Plant A is mushroom and B is *Nepenthes*. Both these plants depend on other organisms for nutrition, i.e. they are heterotrophs.

20. (*c*) Plant *X* is a parasitic plant which derives its nutrition by living in or on the host's body, e.g. *Cuscuta*.

Plant *Z* is an insectivorous plant that feeds on small insects for nutrition. *Y* represents the heterotrophic mode of nutrition where plants depend on other for their nutrition.

21. (*a*) In the given flow chart, *A* could be any autotrophic organisms like green plant, or algae. *B*, *C* and *D* are heterotrophic organisms *A* is *Hydrilla*, which is an autotrophs and does not derive nutrition from other animals. *B* is lichen as they are present in form of naturally beneficial symbiotic relationship between algae and fungi. *C* is *Nepenthes*, an insectivorous plant, which acquire both autotrophic and heterotrophic mode of nutrition. *D* is *Rhizobium*, a saprophyte that derives nutrition from dead and decaying organic matter.

Nutrition in Animals

1. (*c*) *R* and *S* show premolar and molar, respectively. These are specialised for chewing and grinding the food.

2. (*c*) Peristalsis is a wave-like motion generated by rhythmic contraction and relaxation of muscles in wall of oesophagus. This movement helps in passage of food from Mouth → Oesophagus → Stomach.

3. (*b*) Salivary glands in mouth secrete an enzyme called salivary amylase along with the saliva. This enzyme breaks down the starch present in food into maltose (sugar).

4. (*a*) Bile is secreted by the liver. It mainly contains salts, but not any digestive enzymes.

5. (*c*) Bile is a yellowish brown fluid produced by the liver for the digestion of fats in the small intestine.

6. (*d*) Conversion of amino acids into urea does not occur in the stomach, but in another organ (i.e. liver). Rest other options takes place in stomach.

7. (*b*) Protease helps in breakdown of proteins, pepsin is secreated by stomach (*Q*) which helps in digestion of proteins. Further in small intestine(*R*), due to the action of trypsin released by pancreas, digestion of protein completes.

8. (*d*) Part *A* is a pseudopodia, i.e. finger-like projections which encloses the food present in their surroundings. Part *B* is a food vacuole which digests the engulfed food.

9. (*c*) The correct sequence for passage of food through various parts of digestive system are as follows
Mouth → Gullet → Stomach → Duodenum → Ileum → Colon → Rectum → Anus.

10. (*b*) Ruminants are grass eating animals. All statements are correct description of ruminants except IV. The diet rich in carbohydrates, fats and proteins is consumed by human beings. Ruminants have diet rich in plant proteins and cellulose.

11. (*c*) The correct matches are as follows
- Villi are present in small intestine, where they increase its surface area.
- HCL is secreted by stomach lining.
- Bile is secreted by liver.
- Absorption of water takes place in large intestine.
- Mastication is the physical breakdown of food that occurs in our mouth.

12. (*a*) *X* represents villi which are finger-like projections present in small intestine. These structure have thin walls which facilitates efficient absorption of nutrients released from digested food.

13. (*d*) Statement III is incorrect. The correct form of the statement is large intestine absorbs most of the water along with some salt from the food that reaches in it.

14. (*d*) When we eat food, salivary amylase present in our saliva mixes with our food and makes it moistened. Breakdown of protein starts in stomach. In small intestine, all the nutrients such as carbohydrates, proteins, fats are breakdown and absorbed into the blood stream. In large intestine absorption of water and minerals take place.

15. (*c*) Statement I and II are true. The false statement can be corrected as, cellulose cannot be digested in digestive system of human beings (we do not have rumen and lacks digestive enzyme to break cellulose). In the absence of peristalsis, food can still travel down the oesophagus due to the effect of gravity.

16. (*c*) The part labelled *X* is rumen in stomach of ruminants. It is the part where partially chewed food called cud is stored temporarily, Rumen contains anaerobic bacteria which helps in breakdown of cellulose present in grass and green plants.

17. (*a*) Statements I, II, III and V are true. The false statement IV can be corrected as digestion process begins in the mouth of the human digestive system. Here, the teeth breakdown the food into small parts, while tongue lubricates it with saliva for easy passage down in the alimentary canal.

18. (*a*) The temperature of human body is 37ºC. Thus, the salivary amylase enzymes present in saliva will function normally at this temperature only.

19. (*b*) The reactions are completed as,

I. In stomach, Proteins $\xrightarrow{\text{Pepsin}}$ Peptones (smaller fragments of proteins)

II. In small intestine,

III. Starch (carbohydrate) $\xrightarrow[\text{Amylase}]{\text{Pancreatic}}$ Maltose

IV. Fats $\xrightarrow{\text{Bile}}$ Fatty acids and glycerol.

20. (*d*) Digestive juice (II) digested the protein coat completely, hence, it is isolated from small intestine (Y), enzyme (III) partially digested proteins so it must be from stomach (Z).

Enzyme (I) showed no effect on protein coat, so it is most likely collected from the mouth (X).

21. (*c*) B has the highest concentration of dissolved amino acids. It is coming from the small intestine where most of the amino acid are absorbed and are carried to the liver. The blood vessels associated with small intestine carries all absorbed nutrients including amino acids to the liver.

22. (*d*) The part labelled III detects the taste is sour.

23. (*a*) Part X, Y and Z are anus, large intestine and small intestine, respectively.

Option (a) is correct regarding the function of Y, i.e. large intestine.

Fibre to Fabric

1. (*b*) Larvae of silkworm feeds on mulberry leaves. The mulberry silkworms are termed as such because they feed only on mulberry leaves.

2. (*b*) The process of rearing of silkworm to obtain silk is called sericulture. In this process the caterpillars of the domestic silkmoth are the most commonly used silkworm species.

3. (*a*) The fibre obtained from silkworm is made up of protein. During the movement of head, the caterpillar secretes this fibre to make cocoon.

4. (*c*) The given figure is of the cocoon with developing moth inside it. The further development of the pupa into the moth continues inside the cocoon.

5. (*b*) The female silkworm lays about 300 to 400 eggs at a time. She lays eggs on the leaves of mulberry trees. The eggs are covered with gelatinous secretion by which they stick to the leaves.

6. (*c*) At pupa stage, silkworm starts producing silk to form an covering around it called as cocoon.

7. (*b*) Fibre in group I are plant fibres which are obtained from either stem or bud of the plant whereas group II are animal fibre which are obtained either by rearing or shearing of animals.

8. (*b*) Lohi, Marwari and Nali are Indian breed of sheep which provide wool but Changthangi is an Indian breed of goat found in Ladakh.

9. (*b*) Yak wool is commonly found in Tibet and Ladakh. It is produced from the coat hair of the yak.

10. (*c*) Sorter's disease is caused by a bacteria called anthrax. It is a fatal blood disease which is common in workers working in wool industries.

11. (*c*) The removal of grease, dust and dirt from sheared skin with hair in tanks is called scouring. It is the second step of obtaining wool fibre.

12. (*a*) The correct sequence of dyeing process is Shearing → Scouring → Sorting → Dyeing → Straightening.

13. (*c*) Llama is an American breed of camelids. Baluchi is the Pakistani breed of sheep. Bannur is an Indian breed of sheep and Angora is an Indian breed of goat.

14. (*d*) The wool given by Bakharwal sheep is used for making woolen shawls. Bakharwal sheep flocks, spend winter in the Pir Panjal Ranges of the Jammu division, and in the summer migrate to the Kashmir valley.

15. (*a*) Statement I is incorrect because in the process of shearing, no animal (sheep) is harmed. It is a process of removal of fleece of sheep along with thin layer of skin.

16. (*c*) Mulberry, tassar and muga are different type of silk obtained from silkworm. Tassar and muga silk are obtained from cocoons spun by different type of moths. The most common silkmoth is the mulberry silk moth.

17. (*d*) Shearing of sheeps help them to survive in hot weather and Pashmina shawl is obtained from cashmere goat.

18. (*c*) Statement (c) is incorrect. It is corrected as Nylon clothes catch fire easily. Hence, it is advised not to wear nylon clothes while working in kitchen or handling fire.

19. (*c*) Marwari $\longrightarrow$ Coarse wool
Patanwadi $\longrightarrow$ Gujarat
Rampur Bushair $\longrightarrow$ Brown fleece
Nali $\longrightarrow$ Carpet wool

20. (*c*) Weaving is done by using two strand of yarn and knitting is done by using single strand of yarn.

21. (*b*) The female moth lays egg on mulberry leaves through which larva hatch out in 16 days. This larva keeps on molting and start eating mulberry leaves. In 3-8 days the larva fully develop into pupa which start forming silk around it, in 4-6 week. It forms a case around itself, this stage is called cocoon. In next 10 days, the pupa fully develop into adult silk moth.

22. (*d*) *P*-Mulberry silk is known as the most superior quality of silk.
Q-The process of separation of different texture of fibres according to there quality is called grading/sorting.
R-Silk is made up of fibroin protein.
S-Scouring is the process by which sheared skin and hair are washed to remove grease, dirt and dust.

23. (*a*) Hemant and Monika made incorrect statement because *P* is the larval stage of silk moth which feed on mulberry leaves and undergo for moulting.
'*R*' is the protein covering around the pupa which develop into adult moth. It undergoes molting by shedding the protein covering and come out as a fully grown moth. Here, *Q* is the fully grown silkmoth which layeggs.

24. (*a*) *X*-can be silk as it gives off the smell of charred meat and burn slowly. It is the strongest natural fibre whereas *Y*-can be cotton as it burns with yellow flame and on burning it gives off the smell of burning paper. It is the most important cash crop in India.

25. (*c*) *Z*-can be wool fibre which is made up of keratin and *Y*-can be silk made up of fibroin protein.

Heat

1. (*b*) Joule is not a measuring unit of temperature. While kelvin, celsius and fahrenheit are units of temperature.

2. (*a*) The direction of heat flow in the above diagram is from the flask to the ice. Heat flows from higher temperature to lower temperature and temperature of ice is lower than the flask.

3. (*d*) The outer cover and lid of thermos is made of plastic because it prevents loss of heat by radiation.

4. (*d*) The vapours of tea are at higher temperature than the surrounding air. Here air is comparatively at lower temperature can cause the formation of convection currents above the tea. Thus, lead reduces the formation of convection current above the tea.

5. (*d*) Option (d) correctly shows, the convection current of air in a closed beaker when heated.

6. (*b*) In liquids, thermal energy is transferred mainly by convection and this causes change in density. As the liquid is heated the distance between molecules increases. Hence, the density is reduced.

7. (*b*) When water is heated the water near the flame gets hot (i.e., *X*) and hot water rises up (i.e., *Z*). The cold water from the sides moves down towards the source of heat (i.e., *Y*) hence, option (b) is correct.

8. (*c*) The term thermal equilibrium refers to the stage when all the objects involved and the surroundings are at same temperature.

9. (*a*) *E* drop of wax will be melt first due to conduction.

10. (*c*) During summers, iron tracks get heat up by the process of conduction and hence expand. This expansion compensates the gap between the tracks.

11. (*b*) White or shiny surfaces reflect back the heat from the Sun and prevent the fuel to get ignited.

12. (*b*) A clinical thermometer shows a patient's body temperature even after it has been taken out from his mouth because It has a constriction near the bulb, which slows down the mercury flow back to bulb.

13. (*d*) Since, heat flows from higher temperature to lower temperature. So, hot milk will loose heat to the cold water and the temperature of cold water rises.

14. (*a*) The thermometer bulb should be surrounded from all sides by the substance whose temperature is to be measured. Also, the thermometer bulb should not touch the sides or bottom of the container and it should be upright while measuring temperature.

15. (*c*) The bulb should have a thin glass wall so that heat can rapidly reach the mercury in order for the mercury to expand. The bore needs to be narrow in order to increase the sensitivity of the temperature scale. This makes the thermometer to give a faster reading.

16. (*a*) Cutting the food increases its surface area. Greater the surface area, larger the heat loss will be. Hence, heat from the food is lost to the surroundings, so she was able to eat them without burning her tongue.

17. (*a*) Both (i) and (iii) are clinical thermometers used to measure body temperature and (ii) is laboratory thermometer, which can be used for boiling water.

18. (*a*) Since, black is a better absorber of heat, so thermometer A will show higher temperature.

19. (*b*) When she takes baked cake out from the oven it loses heat to the surroundings and cools down.

20. (*a*) Figure (a) indicates the correct method of reading temperature. The thermometer should be hold in front and near to the eyes.

21. (*a*) Expansion rate of mercury is very high and hence, it is used in thermometers. Both clinical and laboratory thermometer have high accuracy. The only difference is that laboratory thermometer measures higher range of temperatures.

22. (*b*) Kink is a narrow and sharp bent in the tube of clinical thermometer.
The range of laboratory thermometer is $-10°C$ to $10°C$.

23. (*d*) Radiation process do not require any medium for transmission of heat.

24. (*b*) Wool is a bad conductor of heat due to which it does not allow heat to transmit to the surroundings.
Water transfers heat by the process of convection.

25. (*c*) The correct order of the thumbtacks according to the time each of them takes to drop from the rod is, Y, X, Z and W because Y is the nearest to candle and W is farthest.

26. (*b*) This is because the two thin blankets joined together will have a layer of air trapped in between them. It prevents the body heat to transfer to the surroundings more efficiently. Hence, it will help to keep the body more warm.

27. (*b*) According to this figure at point 1 the heat is being transfered by convection, at point 2 the heat is being transferred by radiation, at point 3 the heat is being transfered by conduction.

28. (*c*) When a fluid is heated, it expands. Its density decreases and the fluid rises producing convection currents.

29. (*d*) Thermometer P got heated up by radiation and convection method while thermometer Q got heated up by radiation method.

30. (*b*)

Temperature	Degree of hotness
Clinical thermometer	35°C to 42°C
Laboratory thermometer	−10°C to 110°C
Digital thermometer	No mercury
Maximum-minimum thermometer	Weather forecasting

Acids, Bases and Salts

1. (*b*) Oxalic acid is present in spinach (Palak). Ascorbic acid is present in amla and tataric acid is present in unripen grapes.

2. (*c*)   I. The sour things we eat contain acid.
II. Ammonium hydroxide is base.
III. An acid is called organic acid if obtained from animals or plants.
IV. An antacid generally contains a base.

3. (*c*) Antacids are used to neutralise excess acid secreated in the stomach. So, they must be basic. Curd contains lactic acid, so its nature is acidic.

4. (*c*) Magnesium hydroxide and sodium hydrogen carbonate are antacid both are used to cure indigestion. So, the dilute solutions of these are not harmful to drink.

5. (*c*) Lactic acid is present in milk. So, its source is natural. Carbonic acid (H_2CO_3) is a mineral acid. Other two matches are correct.

6. (*c*) The incorrect matching is magnesium hydroxide with whitewash. Magnesium hydroxide is used as an antacid or a laxative in either an oral liquid suspension or chewable tablet form whereas calcium hydroxide and calcium carbonate are used in whitewashing.

7. (*d*) Turmeric is a natural indicator. Colour of turmeric turns red in alkaline/basic medium. The nature of soap solution is basic. So, stain turns red.

8. (*c*) Aqueous solution of blue vitriol is acidic, so it turns blue litmus red.

9. (*a*) $\underset{\text{(Vinegar)}}{2CH_3COOH} + \underset{\text{(Metal oxide)}}{MO} \longrightarrow$

$$\underset{\text{(Water)}}{(CH_3COO)_2M + H_2O}$$

$$(M = \text{Metal})$$

$\underset{\text{(Vinegar)}}{CH_3COOH} + \underset{\text{(Baking soda)}}{NaHCO_3} \longrightarrow$

$$\underset{\text{(Water)}}{CH_3COONa + CO_2 + H_2O}$$

$\underset{\text{(Vinegar)}}{CH_3COOH} + \underset{\text{(Alkali)}}{NaOH} \longrightarrow CH_3COONa + \underset{\text{(Water)}}{H_2O}$

So, the common product she got in the above three experiments is water (H_2O).

10. (*d*) If X is an acid,
(I) it will turn blue litmus red.
(II) shows a pH meter below 7.
(III) release CO_2 with carbonates which turns lime water milky.
(IV) release hydrogen with magnesium ribbon which burns with 'pop' sound.

11. (*d*) Acids react with metals to form poisonous salts. That's why, sour substances like lemon are generally not prescribed to store in metallic containers.

12. (*d*) Inert metals like gold and platinum are soluble in *aqua-regia*. *Aqua-regia* is a mixture of conc. nitric acid and conc. hydrochloric acid in a molar ratio of 1 : 3.

13. (*a*) The indicators among the given substances are red cabbage, turmeric, litmus paper and phenolphthalein.

14. (*c*) Acids as well as bases both are corrosive and their strength is measured in terms of hydrogen ion concentration.

15. (*b*) A turns blue litmus red, so it is an acid. B turns red litmus blue, so it is a base. Common salt (NaCl) is produced when NaOH (base) reacts with hydrochloric acid (HCl).

16. (*b*) Wash the hand immediately with plenty of water which washes away most of the acid and whatever little acid is left is neutralised with the weak base, sodium hydrogen carbonate.

17. (*b*) Solution of common salt is neutral as it is a salt of strong acid and strong base. Thus, it has no effect on blue litmus paper, i.e. blue litmus remains blue.

18. (*c*) Sodium chloride (common salt) is formed by the reaction between hydrochloric acid (an acid) and sodium hydroxide (a base).

$$\underset{\substack{\text{Hydrochloric}\\\text{acid}}}{HCl} + \underset{\substack{\text{Sodium hydroxide}\\\text{(Base)}}}{NaOH} \longrightarrow \underset{\substack{\text{Sodium}\\\text{chloride}\\\text{(Salt)}}}{NaCl} + \underset{\text{Water}}{H_2O}$$

19. (*b*) A should add quicklime to neutralise excessive fertilisers (mainly sulphatic), while B found a supply of washing run off of clothes makes the soil basic, so organic matter is used to neutralise that.

20. (*d*) Mixing of solution of an acid with the solution of base (neutralisation) is exothermic, i.e. temperature increases and salt formation takes place.

21. (*c*) Ant sting injects formic acid. It reacts with baking soda ($NaHCO_3$) of baking powder in following manner:
$$NaHCO_3 + HCOOH \longrightarrow HCOONa$$
$$+ H_2O + CO_2$$

22. (*d*) Limestone - $CaCO_3$
Blue vitriol- $CuSO_4 \cdot 5H_2O$
Washing soda - $Na_2CO_3 \cdot 10H_2O$
Baking soda - $NaHCO_3$

23. (*a*)

Acids	Uses
Hydrochloric acid	As bathroom acid
Sulphuric acid	In storage batteries
Lactic acid	Present in yoghurt
Acetic acid	In making vinegar

24. (*a*) Z produces no colour with phenolphthalein, so, it must be an acidic salt like $CuSO_4$ which is prepared from CuO (basic, i.e. X) and H_2SO_4 (acidic, i.e. Y).

25. (*a*) Salt (P) alongwith water (Q) are obtained when hydrochloric acid (HCl) reacts with sodium hydroxide (NaOH). The process is exothermic (R) and resulting in a neutral (S) solution.

Physical and Chemical Changes

1. (*d*) Shape, size and colour all may be change during a physical change but chemical composition remains the same, e.g. conversion of water into ice.

2. (*c*) Since, melting, boiling and freezing come under the category of physical changes, so *P* must be expansion and *Q* must be physical changes.

3. (*a*) Switching on a light bulb and ironing a wrinkled T-shirt do not result in the change in composition. So, these are the examples of physical changes.

4. (*a*) Physical changes are changes in which a substance undergoes a change in its physical properties. A physical change is reversible. In physical change, no new substance is formed. So, dissolution and crystallisation both are physical, change hence are reversible in nature.

5. (*b*) Burning of coal is a chemical change. Coal burns with air to give carbon dioxide and lot of heat is released during the process, i.e. the process is exothermic.

6. (*c*) When salt is dissolved in water, no change in chemical composition takes place, i.e. it is a physical change and physical changes are generally temporary (i.e. reversible).

7. (*a*) By freezing, water gets converted into ice, which is a solid form of water. In case of solids, force of attraction are more due to which movement of particles decreases.

8. (*d*) All the given may be observed during a chemical change. Chemical changes are those in which new substance is formed and chemical properties are also changed. Chemical changes are irreversible.

9. (*c*) The reason of spoon with a hole is metal reacts with acid present in the pickle to form salt and hence, gets dissolved.

10. (*a*) When iron turning are heated with sulphur powder, a new substance, called iron sulphide is formed. Properties of iron sulphide are quite different from the iron and sulphur individually.

11. (*c*) Rusting is not a crystallisation process. It results in the formation of a new substance, so it is a chemical change. Others are the examples of crystallisation process which is a physical change.

12. (*c*) A chemical change is a permanent change. It always leads to the formation of new substances. However, it may occur with the evolution or absorption of heat. Mixing of oil and water does not affect their chemical composition so, it is a physical change.

13. (*b*) During cooking, respiration and photosynthesis chemical composition of the initial substances change.

14. (*c*) Crystallisation is a temporary change. Digestion and burning both are chemical changes due to the formation of new substances. Such changes are generally irreversible.

15. (*b*) When magnesium ribbon is dissolved in hydrochloric acid, magnesium chloride, a new substance is formed. Similarly, when copper carbonate is heated, it forms black coloured copper oxide, composition of which is quite different from the initial one. So, these two processes are the examples of a chemical change.

16. (*d*) Rusting of iron is a redox reaction. When iron is exposed to the environmental condition, it terribly reacts with water and air and ends up with iron rusting. Iron articles are therefore painted off so that iron cannot react with water and air and they look beautiful by painting with different colours.

17. (*c*) LPG (Liquified Petroleum Gas) is stored at high pressure inside a cylinder. When this gas comes out from the cylinder it experiences a low pressure and it expands. Change-*A* is expansion which is a physical change. Then, it burns in the presence of air to form CO_2 and H_2O. Change *B* is called burnig which is a chemical change.

18. (*b*) In I case, the composition of each wooden log remain the same but in II case, it changes. So I is a physical change while II is a chemical change.

19. (*b*) I is a physical change as kerosene converts from its liquid state to vapour state but have the same chemical composition.
II is a chemical change due to the formation of new substances.

20. (*c*)

A.	Deposition a layer of zinc on iron	Galvanisation
B.	Iron oxide	Rut
C.	Dissolving common salt in water	Physical change
D.	Souring of milk	Chemical change

21. (*d*) Ripening of guava is a slow, chemical, desirable and non-periodic change.

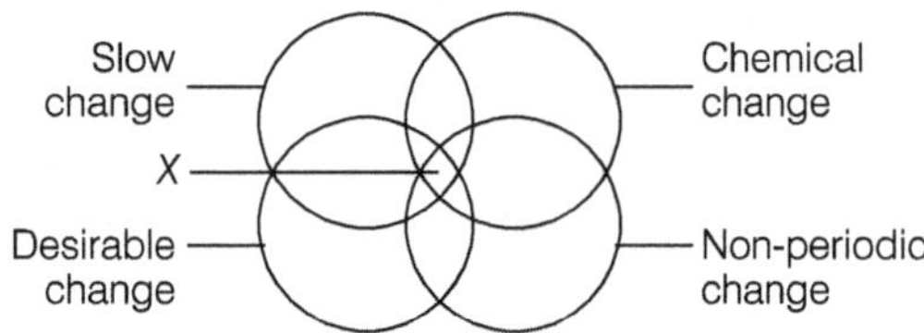

So, X is ripening of guava.

22. (*c*) C part of ship will rust the fastest because it is indirect contact with saline water. So, iron (II) is oxidised into iron (III).

$$Fe(OH)_2 + H_2O + O_2 \longrightarrow Fe(OH)_3$$
$$\underset{\text{hydroxide}}{\underset{\text{Iron(II)}}{}} \qquad \underset{\text{hydroxide}}{\underset{\text{Iron(III)}}{}}$$

23. (*a*) A new substance is formed only in figure *A* and in case of figure *B* no new substance is formed. Process in Fig *A*, it is a chemical change, so in this reaction new compound will be formed and reaction is irreversible, whereas in Fig *B*, crystallisation process take place which is reversible in nature.

24. (*c*)

A.	Heating a metal for expansion	Physical change
B.	Placing a stone in sunlight	Neither physical nor chemical change
C.	Burning of kerosene in stove	Both physical and chemical change
D	Curdling of milk	Chemical change

25. (*b*) When calcium carbonate ($CaCO_3$) react with HCl, it gives calcium chloride ($CaCl_2$), water and CO_2 gas is evolved, which extinguishes candle flame.

$$CaCO_3 + 2HCl \longrightarrow CaCl_2 + H_2O + CO_2(g)$$

Weather, Climate and Adaptations of Animals to Climate

1. (*a*) Desert's climate is very hot and dry. This is due to excess heating and low rainfall in desert regions.

2. (*a*) The region lies in tropics where temperature remain on higher side most of the time and they receive heavy rainfall at regular intervals. Such regions have hot and wet climate.

3. (*b*) As we move away from the equator towards the poles, the temperature will decrease. This happens because the amount of heat received from the Sun decreases and climate becomes cooler.

4. (*b*) The tropics have a hot and humid climate and receive a lot of rainfall. This climate can support a wide variety of flora and fauna and allows them to flourish compared to other climates.

5. (*c*) The animals living in polar regions have a thick layer of fat under their skin which insulates the body of animals against heat loss and also keep them warm.

6. (*d*) Arboreal animals live mostly on trees. These animals should be expert climbers, should be able to eat seeds, leaves, flowers, insects, etc. available on trees. Sharp eyesight helps them to leap accurately between branches. Thus, option (d) is correct.

7. (*a*) Hibernation or winter sleep involves long period of inactivity in organism. The metabolic activity also slows down as body is in state of constant rest.

8. (*c*) A carnivore animal with stripes all over his body who can move very fast, i.e. lion, tiger or similar big cats. These animals are found commonly in tropical rainforests, e.g., Western Ghats in India.

9. (*a*) Lions and elephants both live on the land but they have different food habits. Lions feed on other animals, i.e. it is a carnivores, while elephants are herbivores which prevents any competition for food among these animals.

10. (*b*) Lion and tiger are adapted to live on the land. They have eyes in front of their head which enable them to have a correct idea about the location of their prey.

11. (*c*) Among the adaptive features mentioned, animals living in tropical rainforests show following 4 adaptation, i.e. frugivorous diet, sticky pads on feet, strong tails (e.g. monkey), long and large beaks (e.g. toucan).

12. (*a*) The correct matches are as follows
Wind speed is measured using anemometer.
Air pressure is measured by barometer.
Precipation is measured using a rain gauze.
Temperature is measured using special thermometer.

13. (*b*) Statements I, II and III are false, these can be corrected as
Weather is never constant anywhere. It keeps on changing due to the various effects produced by the Sun's heat.
Humidity is the measure of water vapour in air. Weather is the day to day condition of the atmosphere of a place on daily basis.

14. (*b*) Elephants (*P*) are very large and heavy animal. Its provide stability to animal by spreading its weight over a larger area. Toucan (*Q*) is a bird adapted to find food at the ends of even very thin branches.

15. (*c*) Process *X* is hibernation or winter sleep exhibited by animals such as polar bears. This process helps in escaping the harsh winters of polar region. The metabolic process in body slow down and stored body fat is utilised.

16. (*d*) Migratory birds fly to same location every year. This is probably because they have a built in sense of direction that guides their direction. They may also use the position of Sun at daytime and stars at night to reach their destination.

17. (*c*) In group I, kangaroo rat is a desert animal should be replaced with elephant of group III. This will make all animals in group I from tropical rainforest.
In group II, monkeys should be replaced with seal present in group III (all from polar areas).

Wind, Storms and Cyclone

1. (*c*) Wind causes all the changes in weather.

2. (*a*) Tornadoes are dark funnel-shaped clouds that reaches from the sky to the ground.

3. (*d*) There are three wind belts on Earth, i.e. Polar easterlies, prevailing westerlies and latitude/trade winds.

4. (*b*) Holes are made in hanging banners and hoardings so that the high speed wind can pass through without causing any damage to hoarding or banners.

5. (*d*) Both the evaporation and rise of smoke in air occur because hot air is lighter. Due to rise in temperature molecules expand and occupy more space hence, air become lighter.

6. (*d*) Factors like wind speed, wind direction, temperature and humidity are responsible for the development of cyclone.

7. (*c*) Lightning is discharge of electric charges from the clouds towards the Earth.

8. (*c*) When moving air is rushed to the centre of the storm it forms a very low pressure system and high speed wind revolving around it. This weather condition turns the thunderstorm into a cyclone.

9. (*a*) The tin can get distorted because when the running water is poured on hot can the vapour inside it condenses and the pressure inside the can is lower than the surrounding. Hence, the excess pressure outside the can distorts its shape.

10. (*b*) The forces generated due to Earth's revolution is called Coriolis effect.

11. (*c*) The winds moving from West to East between middle latitude between 30° and 60° are called westerly winds.

12. (*b*) The figure *A* is of anemometer used to determine the speed of wind and the figure *B* is of wind wave used to determine the direction of wind.

13. (*a*) Thunderstorm becomes cyclone when a low pressure is accompanied by high speed winds.

14. (*a*) Increase wind speed is accompanied by decrease pressure and monsoon blows from land towards the sea, in winters.

15. (*c*) *X*-will inflate because when the air inside the balloon heat up the molecules start expanding result in occupying more volume. In other balloons, no heat is absorbed hence, no change in volume is observed.

16. (*d*) Typhoon is an alternative name of cyclone. Anemometer is used to measure speed of the wind. Due to difference in temperature, difference in air pressure in nature is created. Monsoon winds carry water with them. High speed wind is accompanied by low pressure system.

17. (*a*) The bag (*A*) lifted up because on heating the air molecules expand as they absorb heat due to which they exert pressure in upward direction.

Respiration in Human Beings and Animals

1. (*a*) The exchange of gases take place in the lungs (across the membrane of small balloon-like structures called alveoli), i.e. part labelled (*A*).

2. (*b*) The correct passage of O_2 after inhalation through nose is nostrils $\rightarrow$ pharynx $\rightarrow$ trachea $\rightarrow$ bronchi $\rightarrow$ lungs.

3. (c) During heavy exercise, the O_2 is consumed at a faster rate. As a result, glucose is broken down to release energy and lactic acid. The accumulation of lactic acid in muscles cause pain and cramping in legs.

4. (c) In yeast cells, the breakdown of glucose in the absence of oxygen forms alcohol and CO_2 along with release of energy.

5. (a) In insects, oxygen rich air rushes through spiracles into the tracheal tubes, then diffuses into body tissues and reach to every cells present in their body.

6. (b) These events take place during the inhalation of air. Due to contraction of muscles between the ribs, the ribcage moves upward and outward, while the diaphragm move down, air pressure in lungs decreases due to increase in chest cavity and air rushes inside.

7. (a) Breathing in and out in a plastic bag will increase the breathing rate. This happens due to increase in level of CO_2 in bag with every breath. Since no fresh air is available, the O_2 level keeps on decreasing, causing the person to breathe deeply and rapidly.

8. (d) Dilation of arteries and its branches is not responsible for increase in blood flow to skeletal muscles.

9. (b) The increase in blood flow takes place to supply more O_2 to muscles which are actively working. This also removes the heat generated due to rigorous working of muscles.

10. (a) Stomata are tiny openings present on the surface of leaves.
They help in gaseous exchange ($O_2 \rightleftharpoons CO_2$) in plants. The opening and closing of stomata is regulated by guard cells.

11. (d) When a plant is overwatered, it results in expulsion of all the air from between the soil particles. Thus, O_2 is not available to roots and roots start respiring anaerobically. Alcohol is produced as a byproduct whose accumulation can kill the plant.

12. (c) Figure A represents inhalation, while in fig. B it is exhalation. All the statements are correct except (c). In A, i.e. during inhalation, the volume of thoracic cavity will increase and air from outside rushes into lungs.
During exhalation (i.e., B), thoracic cavity decrease in size, as a result the air squeezes out of the lungs.

13. (b) P(intercoastal muscles of ribcage) and Q(diaphragm) both contracts. This increases the volume of thoracic cavity and air from outside (with higher pressure) rushes into the lungs. This process is called inhalation.

14. (c) Different animals uses different types of organs for breathing which suites their structure, habitat, etc. Birds breathe through lungs, cockroach use tracheal for breathing, earthworm respires through skin, dolphin breathe *via* blow holes and fish have gills for respiration.

15. (b) Process A is photosynthesis which uses CO_2 in air and converts it into carbohydrates (i.e. starch), while process B is respiration. Here, carbohydrates, i.e. the energy rich foods get broken into simpler forms in the presence of O_2 and CO_2 is released as waste product.

16. (b) P-Frog respire through moist skin.
Q-Grasshopper respire through spiracles.
R-Fishes respire through gills.
S-*Amoeba* respire through its cell membrane.

Transportation in Animals and Plants

1. (b) This organ is heart located in the chest cavity. Heart beats continuously from the day we are born till the day we die.

2. (b) Kidney is the main organ for eliminating wastes in the form of urine. While skin removes water, excess salts and other small wastes in the form of sweat.

3. (c) If a person cannot produce WBCs, the level of immunity, i.e. the capacity to fight against germs and infections is not present. As a result, the person is prone to random infections.

4. (d) Xylem is a vascular tissue forming a continuous network of channels throughout a plant in order to transport water and minerals absorbed by roots from the soil.

5. (b) During transpiration, plants losses water through stomata. The water moves outwards in form of water vapours.
Thus, when plant was covered with a glass covering, the vapours of water were seen inside the glass cover. It shows that transpiration is taking place.

6. (c) When a potted plant is kept under a fan, the rate of water absorption through the roots will increase. This is because rate of transpiration gets boosted by air.

7. (*d*) The part of root known as root hairs, increases the surface area of the root for absorption of water and dissolved minerals. These hairs are in direct contact with water that remains between soil particles.

8. (*c*) Plasma is the liquid part of blood. It transports CO_2, waste products, hormones and other dissolved substances.

9. (*c*) Part *A* is pulmonary artery which carries deoxygenated (CO_2 rich) blood to the lungs. Part *C* is right ventricle which contains deoxygenated blood returning from all the body parts.

10. (*b*) *R*-Pulmonary artery carries impure blood, i.e., the CO_2 rich blood from heart to the lungs.

11. (*d*) Parts labelled *P, Q, R* and *S* are WBCs, RBCs, platelets and plasma, respectively. Only option (d) is correct for other options, Plasma is the fluid in which all cells are suspended. Platelets helps in clotting to stop loss of blood. WBCs fight against infections and germs causing them.

12. (*c*) The CO_2 rich, i.e. deoxygenated blood flows into the right atrium then to the right ventricle from here blood flows to lungs and O_2 rich blood is sent back to left atrium, then to left ventricle from where it is pumped to body.

13. (*b*) The correct combination is indicated by option (b). For incorrect statement II the correct explanation is -Ureter are a pair of tubes carrying urine from kidney to urinary bladder.

14. (*c*) Stomata are small pores that helps in exchange of gases and in transpiration. Phloem transports food prepared by leaves to all parts of a plant. Hence, option (c) given the correct match.

15. (*b*) Statements IV, V and VI are incorrect. Their correct form is written as transpiration is the process by which, plant losses water through stomata. O_2 is released during photosynthesis. Suction pull helps the water absorbed by roots to climb at great heights.

16. (*b*) The rate of water loss will be maximum in *Y* as water is getting lost by evaporation and transpiration, lower in *Z* as water is lost only by transpiration and zero in *X*. Thus, decreasing order of water loss in three steps is *Y*, *Z* and *X*.

17. (*a*) Aquatic animals excrete ammonia as nitrogenous waste which gets dissolved in large amount of water present in their surroundings. Land animals have less water at their disposal, so they excrete urea as nitrogenous waste.
Birds, insects, reptiles, etc. excrete semisolid, uric acid as waste.

18. (*d*) *X* is a vein. It carries CO_2 rich blood from body parts to heart. Since blood flows at lesser pressure and slowly, their walls are thinner when compared to arteries.

19. (*d*) Only statement (d) is correct. To complete one round of circulation blood enters our heart twice. For incorrect statements, the correct form is written as
- *R*(vein) has valves but *S* (arteries) do not
- In absence of *T*, i.e. capillaries both the nutrient uptake and elimination of wastes will get affected.
- There is no mixing of O_2 and CO_2 rich blood in our heart.

20. (*b*) In movement *Y*-food prepared by leaves is transported to all parts by phloem. In movement *X*-water and minerals gets transported from root to leaves by xylem vessels.

21. (*b*) *P*-is aorta. It carries oxygenated blood from left ventricle to all tissues in the body. *Q*-is pulmonary artery. It carries deoxygenated blood from the heart to lungs. *R*-is pulmonary vein they have valves which allow unidirectional flow of blood. It carries oxygenated blood from the lungs to the left atrium.
S-is septum. It separates the chamber of heart, so that there is no mixing of blood.

22. (*b*) When kept in sunlight for long period of time, more water gets lost than the amount that is being absorbed by the roots at the same time. As a result, the plant wilts.

Reproduction in Plants

1. (*c*) Potatoes are grown by planting modified stems.

2. (*b*) Rhizomes are the main underground stems that bear active buds that can give rise to new plants.

3. (*c*) Rose can be propagated by planting a small cutting of its stem in moist soil. The cutting later on develops roots and shoots and grow into a new plant.

4. (*a*) *X* is the process of cutting, while *Y* is layering. These are the methods of artificial vegetative propagation.

5. (b) Plants like sugarcane, potato, etc. do not produce seeds. They produce new plants by their vegetative parts like stems, roots, buds, etc.

6. (b) X-Spores, i.e. asexual reproductive bodies. Y-Sporangium is knob-like structure carrying spores enclosed within it.

Z-Hypha, is the thread-like projections of the plant.

7. (a) After some time, Nividh can observe that roots and shoot are developing from the eyes of the potato planted in soil. This happens because 'eyes' of the potato are growing regions which can form new plants. Root emerges from bulb and shoot emerges from tuber.

8. (c) The correct sequence of budding in yeast is as follows II, IV, I, V and III.

9. (b) The seed is likely to be dispersed by water, e.g. seeds of lotus or coconut as their seeds are light, spongy and impart ability to float.

10. (c) Part R, i.e. the ovule bears the female gamete in flowers.

11. (d) Potato reproduces from eyes. In the given figure parts labelled Q and S do not have any scars or eyes. Hence, these sections will not produce new plants.

12. (d) Part X is the anther which contains the male gametes called pollens. Part Y is the ovary which contain ovules that form the female gametes.

13. (b) Brightly coloured petals are useful for insect pollinated flowers.

14. (d) For insect pollination, flowers should have nectar as a reward for pollinators, pollen grains and stigma should be sticky, so that they can attach to bodies of insects and get carried away. The gametes should be produced in abundance, so that chances of pollination is enhanced. Thus, A, B and D are correct characteristics of insect pollinated flowers.

15. (a) X-Algae (e.g. *Spirogyra*) which breaks into two or more fragments for reproduction. Y-Turmeric which propagates by buds to form new plants. Z-Moss which reproduces through spores. They lack roots, flowers and seeds.

16. (a) The parts labelled as A-pollen grain, the male gamete. B-pollen tube formed after pollination which carries male gamete to female gamete for fertilisation. C-fertilised egg, formed after fusion of male and female gamete.

17. (b) After fertilisation, formation of embryo take place, the parts of flower fall off except the ovary. Ovary ripens into fruits (P). Ovules develop into seeds and seeds contain embryo (R) covered with seed coat (Q). Endosperm (S) helps in nourishment of developing embryo.

18. (b) Statements II and III are correct. Flower X has pistil, i.e. the female reproductive part, hence, it is a female flower, while Y has both male and female parts, i.e. it's bisexual. Both plants can get pollinated by different methods and perform fertilisation to form seeds and fruits.

Motion and Time

1. (c) The slope of distance- time graph indicates speed of the object.

2. (a) Time taken to complete one
$$\text{oscillation} = AO + OB + BO + OA$$
$$= 0.5 + 0.5 + 0.5 + 0.5$$
$$= 2s$$
Time taken to complete 10 oscillations
$$= 2 \times 10 = 20 \text{ s}$$

3. (a) Distance $= 2\pi r$ (circumference)
$$= 2 \times 3.14 \times 6371 = 40009.88 \text{ km} = 40010 \text{ km}$$

4. (c) $\text{Speed} = \dfrac{\text{Distance}}{\text{Time}} = \dfrac{40010 \text{ km}}{24 \text{ h}}$
$$= 1667.083 \text{ km/h} = 1667 \text{ km/h}$$

5. (d) Distance travelled cannot be decreased with the change in time. It can be either increasing or zero. Hence, graph is not possible.

6. (d) Length of the train (L) = distance travelled by train while crossing Aman
$$L = \text{Speed} \times \text{Time}$$
$$L = 30 \times 3$$
Hence, $\qquad L = 90 \text{ m}$

7. (b) Average speed $= \dfrac{\text{Total distance travelled}}{\text{Total time taken}}$
$$= \frac{100 + 200 + 1000 + 50 + 50 + 100 + 1000 \text{m}}{(5 + 3 + 8 + 2 + 2 + 3 + 8) \times 60 \text{s}}$$
$$= \frac{2500}{1860} = 1.34 \text{ m/s}$$

8. (c) For Ist hour,
$$t = 1 \text{ h}, s = 10 \text{ km/h}$$
So, $d = s \times t = 10 \text{ km}$
For IInd hour,
$$t = 1 \text{ h}, s = 15 \text{ km/h}$$
So, $d = s \times t = 15 \text{ km}$

For IIIrd hour, $t = 1$ h, $s = 20$ km/h
So, $d = s \times t = 20$ km

Total distance travelled $= 10 + 15 + 20 = 45$ km

9. (b) Speed $= \dfrac{\text{Distance}}{\text{Time}} = \dfrac{800}{15} = 53.33 \text{ ms}^{-1}$

10. (d) In a distance time graph a line parallel to time axis represents that the position of the object is not changing with time. Hence, the bike was at rest in this part of the time.

11. (a) Average Speed $= \dfrac{\text{Total distance}}{\text{Total time}} = \dfrac{20}{10}$
$= 2 \text{ ms}^{-1}$

12. (c) The correct statement for both clocks A and B is, time interval of 5 min can be measured by both A and B.

13. (a) The time-period of a simple pendulum is the time taken by it to travel from A to B and back to A.

14. (b) Time-period of a pendulum depends upon its length but independent of the weight of bob. More the length of pendulum, higher will be its time-period.

15. (b) The ratio of distance *versus* speed gives the time taken by an object to cover that distance and to compare the speeds of a number of objects, units need to be same.

16. (b) Circular motion can be uniform when rate of rotation is fixed and the speed of a body changes at every point of the curve to be in circular motion.

17. (a) I. The distance moved by an object per unit time is termed as speed.
II. A moving body changes its position with the passage of time.
III. An object moving along a straight line with constant speed is in uniform motion.
IV. The SI unit of speed is ms^{-1}.
V. The turning of the blades of fan is rotational motion.

18. (a) I. The motion of the Earth around the Sun is a non-uniform motion.
II. The hands of an athlete while running a race are in periodic motion.
III. The speed 36 kmh^{-1} is equivalent to 10 ms^{-1}.
IV. A slower moving object covers a particular distance in longer time as compared to others.
V. Distance travelled by an object is the product of speed of the object to the time taken.

19. (b) A car moving towards North can only have velocity in North direction.

20. (b) Graph I and III are not possible because graph I indicates the time is constant and distance is increasing which is not possible.
Graph III indicates distance is decreasing with the increase in time which is again not possible.

21. (a) I. The slope of distance-time graph gives speed .
II. The time taken by the pendulum to complete one oscillation is called its time-period .
III. The time from one sunrise to the next is a periodic type of motion.
IV. The distance-time graph of a body at rest is a straight line parallel to time axis.
V. If the distance-time graph of a body is a curved line, it represents body is moving with a non-uniform speed.

22. (c) Both statements are correct. If the length of the pendulum is increased, its time-period also increases because time-period of a pendulum depends upon its length. And time-period of a pendulum is always constant for a particular pendulum.

23. (c) I. He is going with high speed that means OA because in this time-period distance rapidly increases.
II. He is going back that means CD because in this time-period distance decreases.
III. He take rest that means BC because it is parallel to time axis.
IV. He slown down that means AB because in this time-period distance increases slowly.

24. (d) A man walks from his home to market with a speed of 5 km/h.
Distance $= 2.5$ km
$\therefore$ Time $= \dfrac{d}{v} = \dfrac{2.5}{5} = \dfrac{1}{2}$ h $= 30$ min
The distance travelled in 10 min.
He returns back with speed of 7.5 km/h in
Distance $= 7.5 \times \dfrac{10}{60} = 1.25$ km
So, average speed $= \dfrac{\text{Total distance}}{\text{Total time}}$
$= \dfrac{(2.5 + 1.25) \text{ km}}{(40/60) \text{ h}}$
$= \dfrac{45}{8}$ km/ h

25. (*b*) Since, for each 5 min, the car is moving a distance of 3 km,

$$\text{Speed} = \frac{3 \text{ km}}{5 \text{ min}} = \frac{3000 \text{ m}}{5 \times 60 \text{ s}} = 10 \text{ m/s}$$

26. (*c*) Average velocity is zero because,

$$\text{Average velocity} = \frac{\text{Total displacement}}{\text{Total time}} = 0$$

27. (*b*) At 7:30 am, the odometer reading of the car
= 28568 km
Speed of the car = 4 km/min
Total time interval between 7:30 am to
9:15 am = 1 h, 45 min = (60 + 45) min
           = 105 min
Required distance = Speed of the car × Time interval
           = 4 × 105 = 420 km
Hence, the odometer reading at 9:15 am
           = 28568 + 420 = 28988 km

Electric Current and Its Effect

1. (*a*) Cotton is an insulator whereas all other are conductor of electricity.

2. (*b*) The correct statement is,
Switch is open, so bulb cannot glow.

3. (*d*) Using a variable resistance, box will help to control the brightness of the bulb in an electric circuit. Here, option (a) show ammeter, (b) shows voltmeter (c) shows resistor and (d) shows, variable resistance.

4. (*b*) Number of cells = $\dfrac{12}{1.5}$ = 8 cells

5. (*a*) In option (a), the position of open key is such that it does not affect the circuit.

6. (*c*) Miniature circuit breaker (MCB) does not work on the heating effect of current.

7. (*d*) The amount of heat produced in a heating element depends on its length, area of cross-section and nature of material.

8. (*b*) Fuse wires are made up of Tin-lead alloy.

9. (*c*) When key is closed, electric current passes through the filament of bulb and it gives heat and light energy.

10. (*c*) The name of the coil of an electromagnet is solenoid.

11. (*b*) An electromagnet is operated on direct current (DC) as power supply.

12. (*d*) The strength of an electromagnet depends upon number of turns in coil, current passing through the coil and nature of core material.

13. (*a*) An electromagnet works only when current is allowed to flow through it.

14. (*b*) If electromagnet is replaced with a bar magnet the bell will ring continuously even without circuit being complete.

15. (*c*) It is an electric bell. It works on the magnetic effect of current.

16. (*c*) An ammeter is always connected in series with the power supply whereas a voltmeter is always connected parallel to the power supply.

17. (*c*) When a switch is in off position, then the circuit is incomplete and hence current does not flow into the circuit.

18. (*a*) I. Current flowing in a wire gives rise to magnetic field around it.
II. The magnet made by using electric current is called electromagnet.
III. A current carrying coil of an insulated wire wrapped around a piece of iron is called solenoid.
IV. Electric bell works on the magnetic effect of current.
V. The safety device based on magnetic effect of current is called MCB.

19. (*a*)

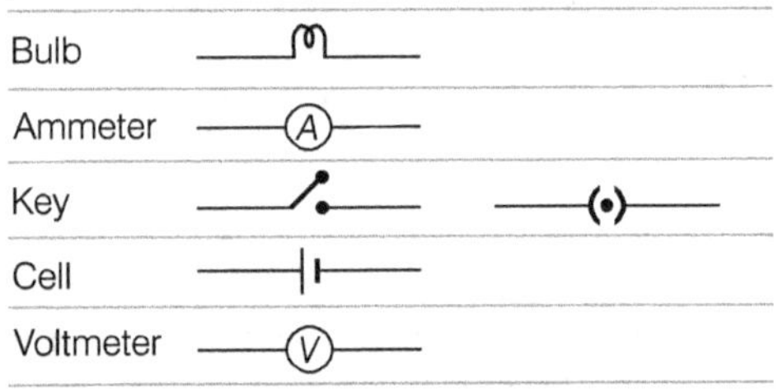

Bulb	
Ammeter	
Key	
Cell	
Voltmeter	

20. (*b*) I. A key or switch in circuit can be placed anywhere in the circuit. Wherever we want to control the components operation.
II. To make a battery of two cells, the longer line is connected to the shorter line of another cell.
III. Household water is a good conductor of electricity because it has charges in the form of impurity, to help the current to flow.
IV. The bulb glows in the circuit only when key is in close position.
V. The SI unit close of electric current is ampere.

21. (*a*) If resistance and current increases in a wire, then heat produced in it also increases. Heating element is made up of nichrome wire and tungsten wire is used in making filament of electric bulb.

22. (*a*) CFL is not based on the magnetic effect of electric current.

23. (*b*) It was observed by Oersted that when a magnetic compass is brought near a current carrying conductor the needle of the compass gets deflected in the direction of flow of electricity.

24. (*a*) Tungsten is a very ductile element and also it catches fire in presence of air when current is passed through it. Nichrome does not expand and can withstand high temperature. Moreover, it does not catch fire in presence of air when current is passed through it.

25. (*a*) Fuse work on heating effect of electric current and electromagnets are used in many devices such as electric bell, cranes etc. Fuses are used to safeguard individual electric devices whereas MCB is used for whole or a major part of the household. Electromagnets can attract all magnetic materials.

26. (*c*) Here statements *C* and *D* are incorrect. Unlike fuses, MCBs are automatic safety switches and need not be replaced. MCB do not serve the same purpose as fuse.

27. (*c*) In an electric bell, electrical energy of supplied electric current is converted into magnetic energy of electromagnet which is further converted into kinetic energy of the gong. This kinetic energy is further converted into sound energy of the bell.

28. (*b*) When the switch of an electric bell is pushed, then a current starts to flow through the electromagnet.

29. (*c*) The correct statement about the circuit is, instrument *Y* measures the voltage of the light bulb and *X* measures the current in the circuit.

30. (*d*) I. A fuse is used for safety purpose in electric circuits.
    II. Fuse wire is made up of an alloy of lead and tin which are in different proportions.
    III. Electric iron works on heating effect of current.
    IV. Connecting many devices to a single socket leads to short-circuit.
    V. If live wire comes in contact with neutral wire, it leads to short-circuit.

31. (*a*) A very high resistive material having low melting point is called a fuse. Filament of bulbs are made up of tungsten. Element of different conducting wires are made up of nichrome. When a large number of appliances are run through a single socket, it leads to overloading and short-circuit.

Light

1. (*c*) The term lateral inversion refers to appearance of left side of object on right side of image and *vice-versa*.

2. (*d*) The image formed by a plane mirror will be virtual, erect and laterally inverted.

3. (*d*) In case of a plane mirror, the object distance is equal to the image distance. So, initially the distance between Geeta and her image is $4 + 4 = 8$ m
   When she moves 1m away, then her image will also move 1m away.
   So, now the distance between her and her image is $8 + 1 \times 2 = 10$ m

4. (*c*) Concave mirror is a spherical mirror and it can form real and inverted as well as virtual and erect images. Dentists rely on concave mirror to cure their patients.

5. (*b*) When a ray of light passes through prism, the deviation of violet light is maximum.

6. (*c*) Splitting of white light into its constituent components is known as dispersion of light.

7. (*b*) Concave lens always form virtual, erect and diminished image.

8. (*b*) The object is moving away from the lens.

9. (*a*) Box *A* converges the rays of light incident on it, so the lens must be converging, i.e. convex lens. Box *B* diverges the rays of light incident on it, so, the lens must be diverging i.e. concave lens.

10. (*b*) The lens is convex lens because it always form real, inverted and diminished image. When the candle is moved closer to lens, the image formed is virtual, erect and magnified.

11. (*b*) Concave lens always forms virtual, erect and diminished images irrespective of the position of object in front of it.

12. (*c*) The inner side of a spoon resembles concave mirror while the other side resembles convex mirror. A convex mirror always form virtual and erect images irrespective of the distance of object from the mirror.

13. (*b*) Convex mirror is a spherical mirror. Its bulging out face perform the reflection. It is used as a rear view mirror in vehicles and it also gives a wide field of view.

14. (*c*) Plane mirrors always form virtual, erect and same size images as that of object and convex mirrors always form virtual, erect and diminished images.

15. (*a*) Correct statement of I is, the incident ray, reflected ray and normal ray always lie on the same plane. Correct statement of II is given in statement III.

16. (*a*) Here, only statement III is incorrect. Lateral inversion is possible only with plane mirrors.

17. (*a*) I. Real images are the one which can be taken on screen.
    II. The image formed in a plane mirror is virtual.
    III. Dentists use concave mirrors to see the infected tooth.
    IV. A periscope works on the principle of reflection of light.
    V. Luminous bodies emit their own light.

18. (*a*) In concave lens, image formed are always diminished.

19. (*c*) I. Convex lens is thicker in middle and thinner at the edges.
    II. Concave lens is also known as diverging lens.

20. (*c*) Lenses work on the refraction of light and lenses are transparent, so light can pass through them.

21. (*c*) Both statements are correct. A rainbow is formed when white light is incident on raindrops and it contains seven colours which undergoes dispersion inside a raindrop.

22. (*a*) I. The image in a concave lens is always smaller than the object.
    II. Convex mirror gives a wide field of view.
    III. It is possible to recombine the lights of seven colours to obtain white light.
    IV. Infrared rays are responsible to give the heating effect in light.
    V. Lenses work on the refraction of light.

23. (*c*) Lenses work on the principle of refraction of light. Convex lens converges the parallel light beam on the focus. Hence, it is called converging lens.

Concave lens diverges the parallel light beam. Hence, it is called diverging lens
Prism disperses light into its seven constituent colours.

24. (*a*) I. The distance of the object from the mirror is equal to the distance of the image from the mirror in case of a plane mirror.
    II. Unlike plane mirror, spherical mirrors donot produce laterally inverted images.
    III. The angle between the normal and reflected ray is the angle of reflection.
    IV. Reflection is the bouncing back of light from a surface.
    V. The nature of images formed by a concave mirror varies with the position of the object.

25. (*a*) I. A magnifying glass is a convex lens used to magnify small objects.
    II. Convex lens is also known as converging lens.
    III. Splitting of light into constituent colours is called dispersion.
    IV. A prism splits sunlight into seven colours.
    V. The band of seven colours of white light is called spectrum.

26. (*b*) A → Incident ray → falls on the surface
    B → Reflected ray → bounce back from the surface
    C → Normal → perpendicular on the surface
    D → Angle of reflection → angle between normal and reflected ray
    E → Angle of incidence → angle between normal and incident ray
    F → Plane mirror → straight reflecting surface

27. (*c*) The light rays reflected from the ball will hit the mirror in the form of incident rays and reflect back to the person's eyes.

28. (*d*) In case of a plane mirror, the object distance and image distance are always equal. Since, *D* is very far away from the mirror, so no image can be seen at *D*.

29. (*c*) We able to see the different colours of the glass because light is reflected into our eyes.

30. (*d*) A prism causes the white light to get dispersed into its constituent components. When a ray passes into the prism, it undergoes refraction. twice. It is because of its non-parallel refracting sides that cause dispersion.

Natural Resources and Their Conservation

1. (*a*) Top soil has the highest amount of organic matter called humus. It is present in *A* horizon.

2. (*c*) Unweathered rocks or parent rocks is the layer in soil profile called bedrock. Here unweathered rocks are present.

3. (*a*) The waste materials which can rot by themselves, i.e., biodegradable do not cause pollution, but non-biodegradable substances like plastics, polythene bags, chemicals like pesticides are soil pollutants.

4. (*c*) Clayey soil has the highest water retention followed by loamy and the sandy soil cannot hold any water.

5. (*c*) Sandy soil contains large sized soil particles which allows air to reach these spaces in soil. As a result sandy soil is well-aerated.

6. (*a*) Percolation rate $= \dfrac{\text{amount of water (mL)}}{\text{percolation time (min)}}$
$= \dfrac{500}{30} = 16.6 \text{ mL / min}$

7. (*d*) Sandy soil will allow the percolation of water from surface to underground areas at the fastest rate. This is because of large space pockets between soil particles which are unable to retain water.

8. (*a*) In the grit and sand removal tank solid and heavy objects like sand, grit, pebbles and stones, etc. are allowed to settle at the bottom of tank which are removed later.

9. (*a*) Untreated human excreta is a health hazard as it contains many disease causing microbes and pollutants that can contaminate both soil and water bodies. This polluted water when consumed by people can cause harmful diseases like typhoid and cholera.

10. (*b*) In soil where clay content is higher, water logging is a problem. The little space present between clayey soil particles gets occupied by water thus pushing out the O_2. As a result roots cannot receive O_2 and die out.

11. (*c*) To reduce water pollution we should not excrete in open, as this waste ultimately gets added to nearby water bodies, excess spraying of fertilisers in crop field will lead to water pollution, construction of more pukka floor will reduce infilteration process and water level will seep into the ground.

Proper disposal of waste in sewer lines/system is the only method to reduce water pollution given here.

12. (*a*) The state of water at *P* will be vapours. This is because water is loss in form of water vapours from the leaves during transpiration as vapour similar to evaporation.
At *Q*, water is in liquid form as the vapour condenses and form water droplets which falls to the ground.

13. (*d*) Ozone is a protective layer of our atmosphere which absorbs harmful UV rays from entering the Earth's surface. Its chemical form is also used to disinfect the treated wastewater. It kills any microbes present in the water.

14. (*a*) For cotton, sandy or loamy soil which drain water easily and holds plenty of air is suitable. Cotton grows best in black soil.

15. (*b*) The process *Y* is identified as evaporation. It involves changing of water into vapour.

16. (*a*) The readily usable water available for humans occurs in the form of groundwater, aquifers, rivers and freshwater lakes.

17. (*b*) The sources of water that is available to humans is groundwater, aquifers, rivers and freshwater lakes.
Water found below the water table is called groundwater. It is found under the ground in the cracks of spaces in soil, sand and rock. Seeping of water into the ground is known as infiltration.
When a water-bearing rock readily transmits water to wells and springs, it is called as an aquifer. Bawris were deep step wells built into the ground. It was the traditional way of rainwater harvesting. These were built to store rainwater.

18. (*c*) A sewage treatment plants involves Bar screen followed by grit and sand removal tank which is further followed by sedimentation and aeration tank, respectively and lastly sludge digester during the processing of waste water.

19. (*b*) The process marked in the figure are
   1. groundwater   2. evaporation
   3. condensation   4. clouds
   5. transpiration   6. precipitation
The statements I-IV currently matches as
I-(2), II-(1), III-(3), IV-(6)

20. (c) $S \rightarrow$ Humus, organic substance made from dead leaves

$R \rightarrow$ Clay, whose particles are compactly packed and have little air.

$Q \rightarrow$ Sand, granular material composed of finely divided rocks.

$P \rightarrow$ Gravel is a loose aggregation of rock fragments.

21. (b) Proportion of fine and large particles is equal. Desalination is not an effect of soil erosion.

It is a method of taking away minerals components from saline water.

22. (b) The figure represents drip irrigation. It is a method of watering agricultural fields with the help of arrive tubings to deliver water directly at the base of plants.

Forests

1. (a) When forest is destroyed, the ecosystem of the region also gets destructed.

2. (c) Recycling the paper waste, e.g. bags, envelope, etc. can help in conservation of trees. This is because papers are derived from trees.

3. (d) Forests maintain the balance between O_2 and CO_2 in the atmosphere. They absorb CO_2 and produce O_2 (in photosynthesis). Thus, if all forests disappear, the level of CO_2 in atmosphere will increase.

4. (b) Oxygen is not produced by the action of decomposers.

5. (c) The layer is canopy where trees of height approx. 100 feet are found which stops most of the sunlight and rain from reaching the ground.

6. (b) Primary consumers are the animals who directly feeds on the producers, i.e. the green plants. Thus, goat, rabbit and horses are all primary consumers.

7. (a) For a food chain, it is essential to have following components, i.e. producers $\rightarrow$ primary consumer $\rightarrow$ secondary consumer and so on. Every food chain begins with a producer, i.e. a green plant. Thus, option (a) is correct.

8. (c) In the given food chain, X will be occupied by a herbivore animal which feeds on grass. Hence, the correct option is deer.

9. (b) The increase in level of CO_2 is a result of cutting down of rainforests which adds high amount of CO_2 in the atmosphere. Burning of fossil fuel also adds to higher level of CO_2 in the atmosphere.

10. (a) Forests play a vital role in the preservation of water cycle. It also maintains the climate of area with the help of transpiration, photosynthesis, etc.

11. (a) In the food chain, (i) a green plant known as producer, (ii) is a primary consumer or a herbivore which feeds on producer, (iii) is a secondary consumer and (iv) is a top level carnivore.

12. (a) X consumes all other organisms in this food web. This is possible when X is a decomposer, as it would be able to consume dead organic matter from all other organisms.

13. (b) X shows exchange of gases in plants take place through stomata, whereas transpiration is a process in which plant lose water in form of vapours through stomata. Y represents respiration process in which CO_2 is released by animals.

14. (c) Branched part of a tree above the stem is called as crown. Decomposers enable the nutrients present in dead animals and plants remains to return back to soil.

Practice Set 1

1. (b) Since, both bicycles are approaching with same speed. So, they both will cover same distance before hitting each other.

$$\text{Distance covered} = \frac{60}{2} = 30 \, \text{km}$$

$$\text{Speed} = 15 \, \text{km/h}$$

$$\text{Time taken} = \frac{\text{Distance}}{\text{Speed}} = \frac{30}{15} = 2 \, \text{h}$$

2. (a) Colour of turmeric is yellow in acidic medium and red in basic medium. Since, solution of baking soda and lime water are basic in nature, therefore it gives red colour with turmeric whereas solution of lemon juice is acidic in nature therefore the colour remains yellow same in case of neutral solution of common salt.

3. (c) The blood brings wastes to the kidney through the renal artery. Nephrons purify the blood and clean blood flows out of the kidneys through the renal vein.

4. (d) According to second law of reflection, angle of incidence is always equal to the angle of reflection. i.e $\angle i = \angle r$

Here, $\angle i = 70°$

So, $\angle r = 70°$

5. (*a*) Chemical change involves change in chemical composition which remain unaffected in case of physical change. Thus, beating of aluminium foil and cutting of wood log are the examples of physical changes while remaining two are the chemical changes.

6. (*d*) Wasp sting inject some base, which can be neutralised by some acid.
Appearance of green colour of litmus paper shows the neutral nature of a solution.
Salts of nitric acid are called nitrates, e.g. $NaNO_3$ (sodium nitrate).

7. (*b*) Time taken $= 15$ min $= 15 \times 60$ s

Speed $= 70$ km/h $= 70 \times \dfrac{5}{18}$ ms^{-1}

Distance $=$ Speed $\times$ time

$= 70 \times \dfrac{5}{18} \times 15 \times 60 = 17500$ m

$= 17.5$ km

8. (*b*) Time taken $= 10$ min $= 10 \times 60$ s $= 600$ s

Distance $= 17500$ m

Speed $= \dfrac{Distance}{Time} = \dfrac{17500}{600} \times \dfrac{18}{5}$ km/h

$= 105$ km/h

9. (*c*) Distance $= 17500$ m $= 17.5$ km

Speed $= 50$ km/h

Time $= \dfrac{Distance}{Speed} = \dfrac{17.5}{50} = 0.35$ h

$= 0.35 \times 60$ min $= 21$ min

$8:15$ am $- 21$ min $= 7:54$ am

10. (*c*) Ceramic and glass are insulators whereas copper and graphite are conductors. In case of option (c), circuit is complete with the bulb even if insulators are connected in parallel.

11. (*d*) The image formed by a converging lens can be real or erect depending upon the distance between the object and surface of lens. Real image formed by convex lens are inverted in nature, whereas virtual image is also formed by convex lens which is erect and larger in size.

12. (*d*) During a chemical change, a new substance is formed. Since, Z is quite different from X and Y, so it is a chemical change.

13. (*a*) Total incoming current will always be equal to outgoing current. Henc, current in PR will be $RS - QR$

$= 5$ A $- 2$A $= 3$ A

14. (*b*) In case of beaker Y, heat energy will be more. Because more water will acquire more heat energy.

15. (*b*) Combustion, curd formation and digestion all involve change in chemical composition, so these are the examples of chemical changes. All these are irreversible processes. Crystallisation is a reversible process but no new substance is formed during this process.

16. (*a*) Sunlight is trapped with the help of chlorophyll in plants and carbon dioxide is taken up by stomata of leaves.
Cuscuta is an example of a parasite as it takes shelter in a host plant and absorb food material from it.

17. (*a*) Litmus paper is blue when pH is more than 7. Thus, at point A.

18. (*b*) At 20 mL of Y, pH of X becomes 7. Hence, 20 mL of Y neutralises the liquid X.

19. (*b*) It shows excess of Y after neutralisation of X completely.

20. (*c*) For respiration, plants use oxygen and release carbon dioxide, whereas for the purpose of photosynthesis they use carbon dioxide and release oxygen. Respiration is a chemical process which involve release of heat energy by breakdown of organic compounds.

21. (*a*) $M \rightarrow$ Canines
$N \rightarrow$ Incisors
$Q \rightarrow$ Premolars
$P \rightarrow$ Molars
P is molars as they are present in 12 in number in adults but 8 in number in children, whereas Q are premolars which are absent in young children but 8 in number in adults.

22. (*c*) The temperature of ice $= 0°C$

Obtained reading $= 2°C$
So, error in thermometer $= 2°C$
Hence, actual temperature of glass of water at room temperature $=$ Obtained reading $-$ error
$= 30°C - 2°C = 28°C$

23. (*a*) Dilute solution of mineral ions act as a hypotonic solution which leads to movement of water molecules into the root hair by osmosis.

24. (*a*) Hydrochloric acid + Sodium hydroxide $\rightarrow$ Sodium chloride (Neutral salt) + water.
In the reaction, new substance are formed hence, the arrangement of atoms does not remain the same.

25. (*c*) By flooding the land with saline water cyclone decreases the fertility of the soil in the coastal areas.

26. (*d*) Heat starts flowing from the substance to water until both the substance and water reaches the same temperature. Hence, temperature of the system will be in between 30°C and 60°C.

27. (*d*) A hot air balloon goes up because the air inside the balloon is heated up which causes the air to rise up. Now, the rising air applies a pressure on the walls of the balloon which pushes the balloon upwards.

28. (*c*) Aerobic respiration takes place in the presence of oxygen. When muscle contracts, energy is used, this energy is supplied by the oxidation of glucose to release carbon dioxide and water.

29. (*b*) Clayey soil has highest water holding capacity.

30. (*c*) The time period of oscillation of a pendulum does not depend on the mass of the pendulum. Hence, time period for both pendulums will be the same.

31. (*d*) In an electric bell, when the key is pushed, the coil inside it behave like an electromagnet and armature is attracted towards the coil and the clapper strikes the gong and produce sound.

32. (*c*) Ammonium chloride forms white vapours on heating which get deposited on the upper cooler part of test tube.

33. (*d*) (I) is moving with constant speed but (II) is not in motion because distance remains same with increase in time.

34. (*b*) Pollination takes place at stigma whereas fertilisation takes place in ovary.

35. (*b*) The left ventricle has the highest pressure in order to pump blood throughout the body except to the lungs. The right ventricle pumps blood to the lungs only therefore requires less pressure.

36. (*a*) Cotton and flax are plant fibres, wool and silk are animal fibres and polyester and rayon are synthetic fibres.

37. (*b*) If an object placed at the centre of curvature of a concave mirror, then the image will be formed at the centre of curvature itself.

38. (*b*) The cells are white blood cells, they help the body to fight against infections.

39. (*b*) In winter, the wind blows from land towards the ocean and in summer the winds blows from the ocean towards the land.

40. (*b*) Iron nails kept in copper sulphate solution, displace copper from the solution and form iron sulphate solution.

$$\underset{\text{(Iron)}}{\text{Fe}} + \underset{\substack{\text{(Copper sulphate}\\\text{solution)}}}{\text{CuSO}_4} \longrightarrow \underset{\text{(Copper)}}{\text{Cu}} + \underset{\substack{\text{(Iron sulphate}\\\text{solution)}}}{\text{FeSO}_4}$$

This is an example of displacement reaction.

41. (*c*) Figure (c), correctly shows the direction of the convection current when water is heated.

42. (*b*) Mode of reproduction in plants is both sexual and asexual. New organisms can formed or reproduces sexually as well as asexually.

43. (*d*) Voltmeter is a device used to measure voltage across any component. It is connected in the parallel to the component.
A key is a device used to control the circuit by switching it on or off.

44. (*c*) Litmus turns into red colour in acidic solution whereas it turns into blue in alkaline solution. Hence, lemon is acidic and alkaline in nature.

45. (*b*) Statement II is incorrect becauses WBC's (white blood cells) fight against the foreign particles that may harm our body.

46. (*d*) Conduction and convection require medium to transfer heat. They cannot happen in a vacuum and only radiation can pass through a vacuum.

47. (*a*) Opening and closing of stomata is done by guard cells, fluid matrix in the chloroplast is called stroma, xylem are tiny vessels that transport water from roots to all parts whereas phloem transport food from leaves to different parts of plants. Edges of leaves are part of lamina.

48. (*c*) East coast of India is more vulnerable to cyclonic storm and an eastward shift in the wind current is observed due to rotation of Earth.

49. (*c*) Fertilisers, cattle dung and compost add nutrients to soil and improve its quality. Nitrogen fixing leguminous crops also helps in soil improvement.

50. (*c*) *A* is chloroplast containing chlorophyll which helps in capturing energy from sunlight for the process of photosynthesis.
B is guard cells which helps in opening and closing of stomata. (*C*)

Practice Set 2

1. (a) Average speed $= \dfrac{2000}{5 \times 60} \text{ ms}^{-1}$

$= \dfrac{2000}{5 \times 60} \times \dfrac{18}{5} \text{ km/h} = 24 \text{ km/h}$

2. (a) Phloem is the vascular tissue responsible for transporting organic nutrients around the plant body. It carries dissolved sugars from the leaves to other parts of the plants.

3. (d) Average speed $= \dfrac{\text{Total distance}}{\text{Total time}}$

$= \dfrac{20}{4 \times 60} = 0.08 \text{ ms}^{-1}$

4. (c) Mishri is in the form of large crystals. Galvanisation is the process of deposition of a thin layer of zinc over iron to protect it from rusting. Souring of milk is a chemical change whereas dissolution is a physical change. Iron oxide (hydrated) is called rust. CO_2 turns lime water milky.

5. (c) Both concave and convex mirror form virtual images. A convex mirror always form virtual image, while a concave mirror form virtual image, of an object placed very close to the mirror.

6. (c) When one litre water at 20°C is mixed with one litre water at 60°C. The hot water at 60°C exchange heat with cold water at 20°C. The final temperature is between 20° and 60°C.

7. (b) Jantra Mantra, use sundial to measure time which uses the position of the sun and the direction of the shadows to tell time in the ancient days. As, the position of sun changes in the sky, the position of shadow of blade on the dial also changes. This position of shadow of vertical blade on the dial gives the time of the day.

8. (c) In ancient time, position of Sun and Moon in the sky is used to measure time in day and night.

9. (c) Average speed of car $= \dfrac{\text{Total distance}}{\text{Total time}}$

$= \dfrac{(500 + 490) \text{ km}}{(10 + 7) \text{ h}} = 58.24 \text{ km/h}$

10. (b) The regular vibrations of quartz crystal when connected to an electric circuit is used to measure time very accurately.

11. (d) Since, glass is optically denser medium. So, ray will bend towards the normal.

12. (c) When light changes its medium, it bends towards the normal if medium is denser and away from the normal if medium is rarer. Hence, option (c) is incorrect because no refraction of light occurs.

13. (a) Magnesium burns with dazzling white light and oxygen is necessary for combustion. Magnesium oxide (MgO) is formed when oxygen reacts with magnesium.

14. (c) In alkaline medium, colour of phenolphthalein is pink, whereas it is colourless in acidic medium.

15. (b) 30 cm corresponds to $-10°$-$110°C$

$\Rightarrow$ 30 cm is equivalent to 120 readings.
So, 1 cm $\Rightarrow 120/30$ readings = 4 readings and 20 cm $\Rightarrow 4 \times 20 = 80$ readings
Temperature at which the mercury thread would be 20cm long is $\Rightarrow 80 - 10 = 70°C$

16. (b) When the bulbs are connected in parallel circuit, then overall resistance decreases because of which brightness of the bulb increases.

17. (c) Most of the times the waste coming from the factories is acidic and may kill aquatic life, so its neutralisation is necessary.

18. (c) The angle between reflected ray and normal at the point of incidence is known as angle of reflection.

19. (c) Fuse is an electrical safety device that operates to provides overcurrent protection of an electrical circuit.

20. (d) Earthworms exchange gases through their skin *via* diffusion. This type of respiration is known as cutaneous respiration or skin breathing.

21. (b) When sea water is heated below its boiling point, water evaporates leaving the salt as residue. This process is called evaporation.

22. (d) During neutralisation process, acid as well as alkali loses its properties. The pH of acid increases while that of alkali decreases.

23. (d) The colour of the leaves and height of the seedlings are both characteristics of the seedlings that Mannu observed to tell which pot of plant was growing better.

24. (b) In figure (b) the direction of magnetic field lines are correct. The lines start from North pole and end on South pole. The lines always make a complete loop.

25. (c) The cooking utensils are always fitted with plastic handles because plastics are poor thermal conductor. Thus, it protects our hands from burn.

26. (*a*) Food molecules are digested to become small molecules of glucose by the action of carbohydrase (*P*) and become amino acid by the action of protease (*Q*).

27. (*b*) In *B* part of the digestive system, hydrochloric acid is produced.

28. (*a*) Rubber shoes prevent us from getting electric shock because rubber is a very good insulator.

29. (*d*) When you stand on bare feet with one foot on a stone floor and the other on a carpet, the stone floor feels colder than the carpet because more heat energy flows from your foot to the stone floor than from your foot to the carpet.

30. (*d*) Phloem is the structural component of plants. It is made up of living cells and helps in transportation of food from leaves to all parts of plant through its various components including sieve plates.

31. (*b*) Metal *Y* is better conductor of heat because after heating the length of *Y* strip increases more then the metal *X*.

32. (*c*) Common name of hydrochloric acid is muriatic acid.

33. (*c*) Acids and alkalis are hazardous when concentrated, both are colourless liquids and contain water.

34. (*c*) Arrow *A* represents, absorption of water and minerals by the roots from the soil.

35. (*a*) There are two process involved here are conduction and melting on heating, the test tube transfer heat in the water (conduction) due to which ice converts into water (melting).

36. (*b*) The cause is that the bodies of the ships are in contact of salty water, and solution is galvanisation. By galvanisation a thin layer of zinc is deposited on the iron and hence the rusting is prevented.

37. (*b*) Statements II and III are true because the tea in the three glasses are at the same temperature, i.e. 75°C and there is more heat in glass *A* than in glass *B*.

38. (*d*) Silver and copper are very good conductors of heat. Iron is worst among the given for the conduction of heat.

39. (*d*) The ammeter reading in the all three circuits are same because the arrangement of a cell, a resistor a key and an ammeter is same.

40. (*a*) Trade winds flows towards the equator from the North-East in northern hemisphere or from the South-East in southern hemisphere. These are also known as tropical easterlies.

41. (*a*) Location of the three types of cell is
$P \rightarrow$ Epidermis; $Q \rightarrow$ Cortex
$R \rightarrow$ Primary phloem; $S \rightarrow$ Primary xylem
Epidermis (*P*) protects the underlying cells. Cortex (*Q*) contains stored carbohydrates or other substances such as resins, latex, essential oils and tannis. Primary phloem (*R*) transport organic nutrient, (sucrose) to all parts of the plant. Primary xylem (*S*) transport water in plants.

42. (*b*) The figure shows systolic condition. Both atrio-ventricular valves, i.e., tricuspid (3) and mitral valves (4) are closed and the aortic (2) and pulmonary (1) valves are open.

43. (*b*) The method of reproduction which involve single parent to produce offsping is called asexual reproduction. Budding, spore formation, regeneration and fragmentation are types of asexual reproduction performed by *Hydra*, fungi, *Planaria* and Sea anemone, respectively.

44. (*d*) Anaerobic respiration takes place in plants in the presence of little or no O_2, e.g. roots of plants in water logged condition.

45. (*b*) In case of figure (ii), all the components are connected properly. i.e. ammeter is connected in series and voltmeter is connected in parallel.

46. (*a*) Mushroom is a fungi that is saprophytic in nature. It gets its food from dead and decaying plants.

47. (*a*) *P* is stamen, it contains pollen grains and *Q* is carpel, its lower part is ovary that contains ovule.

48. (*a*) Cutting vegetables is a physical change as it does not change chemical composition whereas change in colour is a chemical change. It is an irreversible change.

49. (*c*) Root hair absorb water that means, water enters into xylem vessels through root hair, where vessels are formed by dead cells and the root hair lie in between soil particles and cells of xylem vessels are joined with open ends.

50. (*b*) Lid expands more than the neck and thus slides easily. As lid is made up of metal that expand on heating whereas neck of bottle is of glass which show no effect on heating.

www.ingramcontent.com/pod-product-compliance
Lightning Source LLC
LaVergne TN
LVHW080723170726
843469LV00082B/1902